-0. JAN. 1979

D1549739

THE ANCIENT GREEKS
HOW THEY LIVED AND WORKED

POPE   938   7507727

Please renew/return this item by the last date shown.

So that your telephone call is charged at local rate, please call the numbers as set out below:

	From Area codes 01923 or 0208:	From the rest of Herts:
Renewals:	01923 471373	01438 737373
Enquiries:	01923 471333	01438 737333
Minicom:	01923 471599	01438 737599

Hertfordshire
COUNTY COUNCIL
Community Information

1 3 SEP 2005
- 2 FEB 2007
- 9 NOV 2009
2/12

L32a

Uniform with this book

The Ancient Romans: How They Lived and Worked
by O. A. W. Dilke

The Ancient Greeks

HOW THEY LIVED AND WORKED

Maurice Pope

7507727

DAVID & CHARLES
NEWTON ABBOT LONDON

ISBN 0 7153 7081 2

© Maurice Pope 1976

All rights reserved. No part of this
publication may be reproduced, stored
in a retrieval system, or transmitted,
in any form or by any means, electronic,
mechanical, photocopying, recording or
otherwise, without the prior permission
of David & Charles (Publishers) Limited

HERTFORDSHIRE
LIBRARY SERVICE

938   16 AUG 1976

7507727

Set in 11pt Baskerville, 2pt leaded
and printed in Great Britain by
Latimer Trend & Company Ltd Plymouth
for David & Charles (Publishers) Limited
Brunel House Newton Abbot Devon

Contents

Contents

Illustrations

Preface

THE ancient Greeks were so original in themselves and so influential in the history of human civilisation that everybody is interested in them. But their achievements were so varied that not everybody is interested in them all in the same degree or in the same order of priority. I have tried to take this into account and to make each of my chapters an independent tour, intelligible in itself. The reader can choose which to take when, but if he wants the traditional approach of an historical survey, he should begin at the beginning.

The title of the book is enough to indicate that it does not seek to explore the peaks of Greek discovery in art, literature, philosophy, science, or mathematics, only the practical success with which they organised their lives and from which their more lasting achievements grew. Even so, nobody will expect the exploration to be exhaustive. However, those who wish to find out more or to check what they are told will find the means to do so in the Sources (pp 160–64).

My main debt of gratitude is to Professor O. A. W. Dilke, the author of the companion volume, *The Ancient Romans*, who not only suggested that I wrote the book in the first place but read and commented in detail on my first draft. George Forrest of Wadham College, Oxford, read the whole of the completed manuscript, and I should like to thank him for the many welcome and useful suggestions he made. I also received much kindness and help from the officials of the various museums and other institutions which have supplied me with illustrations. Finally I must thank the publishers of the book, David & Charles, for their patience and encouragement.

M.P.

A Note on Ancient Greek Money

METAL, measured by weight, was the normal medium of exchange in the Bronze Age. Coinage is said to have originated in Lydia, and was perhaps first devised as a ready means of paying troops, the stamp guaranteeing both the purity and the weight of the metal. However that may be, the idea was taken up by an increasing number of Greek city-states in the seventh and sixth centuries BC.

The plate on p 104 illustrates some important issues:

(a) An Aeginetan 'tortoise', a double drachma (F) of the late sixth century BC. Silver. Aegina was probably the first city in Europe to strike coins, beginning in the early seventh century and continuing till her defeat and annexation by Athens in 456 BC. The obverse alone bears a device.

(b) Two everyday silver coins of classical Athens, a drachma (E) and an obol (D). On the obverse is the head of Athena, on the reverse an owl, an olive branch, and the Greek letters for A TH E.

(c) A Persian gold daric (B) of the fifth century BC. On the obverse is the king with a bow in his left hand and a spear in his right. The reverse has no design. First issued by Darius the Great (522–485 BC), these coins circulated widely in Greece as well as in the Persian Empire. They were approximately twice the weight of an Athenian drachma, and more than twenty times its value.

(d) An electrum stater (C) of Cyzicus. On the obverse is a lyre, and beneath it a tunny-fish, which was a main factor in the city's prosperity and which figured on all its coins. The reverse has no device but incuse depressions in a four-square pattern. Cyzican staters were a principal medium of exchange in the Athenian grain trade with the Black Sea ports during the fourth century BC.

9

(e)   Gold stater (A) of Philip II of Macedon (359–336 BC). Head of Apollo on the obverse, and on the reverse Philip's name below a racing chariot and a symbolic trident.

(f)   Bronze coin (G) of Hiero II of Syracuse (275–216 BC). On the obverse is the head of Hiero wearing a diadem, and on the reverse a helmeted horseman with a flowing cape (*chlamys*) over his cuirass and holding a spear. Below is the king's name in the genitive case IERONOS.

(g)   Silver four-drachma piece (H) of Menander, the ruler of Greek India, 167–c147 BC. Menander helmeted on the obverse, and on the reverse the goddess Athena. The coin bears the legend 'King Menander the Saviour' in both Greek and Indian.

Athenian money was reckoned as follows:

8 *chalkoi* ('coppers')	= 1 obol
6 obols	= 1 drachma
100 drachmae	= 1 mina
60 minae	= 1 talent of silver

An Athenian talent was about 26kg of silver, but standards differed between cities in the same way as the gallon differs between the United States and Britain. In Aegina for instance a talent was 37·8kg.

It is impossible to give any accurate translation of ancient money into modern terms. One drachma was a standard day's pay in classical times, and we are told in a speech from the law courts of the fourth century BC that a capital of 45 minae (which at 8 per cent would yield a drachma a day) was 'only just enough to live on'. The interest on a talent was considered adequate to maintain and educate a child. We hear of houses in Athens costing from 9 to 44 minae. Theatre tickets cost 2 obols. So as a rough aid to the imagination we may think of an Athenian obol in 400 BC as being worth about the same as an English pound or US $2.50 in 1975.

I

Introducing the Ancient Greeks

Their name

THE Greeks call themselves Hellenes and their country Hellas. They have done so for 2,500 years, since the sixth or seventh century BC. Before then they do not seem to have had a single name for themselves, only for their different tribes and subdivisions. In the east their country is still called after one of them: Javan in Hebrew (found in our Bible) and Yunan or Yunani in Arabic, Persian, and Turkish, all come from 'Iawones', which is how the Ionians ('Iones' in classical Greek) once pronounced their name.

Our own name for the Greeks, shared with all other western European languages, comes from the Latin 'Graeci'. We know little or nothing about who the 'Graeci' were, except that they were not an important part of the Greek people as the Ionians had been. Presumably they were just the first Greek speakers that the Romans came across. However, their name has stayed with us, and though the attempt is sometimes made by purists to have it replaced by Hellenes, it still seems unnatural in English to call the Greeks anything but Greek.

Their home

Modern Greece is a country of some 50,000 square miles, comprising the southern part of the Balkan peninsula and the islands of the Aegean and the south Adriatic. In antiquity, and indeed until 1922, when an exchange of populations was effected with Turkey, the Greeks lived also on the east coast of Asia Minor. In Sicily, too, and round the whole of the southern

Map of Greece

part of Italy, there were so many Greek cities that the area was called 'Greater Greece'. But they were the product of early colonisation. The homeland of the Greeks was, as it still is, the southern Aegean.

Their history

There was a Bronze Age civilisation in Greece of considerable splendour, though it is not certain how much of it was Greek-speaking. Some memory of the period survived into historical times, but it has not left any direct literary record of itself, and our knowledge of it is almost entirely based on archaeological discovery. At the end of the second millennium BC there was a marked decline in material standards, and probably a great fall in population. We know very little about what life was like in Greece for the next two or three hundred years. In the eighth century BC a revival took place, and Greek history as opposed to prehistory can be said to begin then. There was prosperity, expansion, and experiment in all directions.

This new Greek civilisation reached the climax of its glory in the fifth century BC and of its power in the fourth, when virtually the whole world from South Italy to the Himalayas, and from Egypt to the Crimea, came under Greek control. Later Greeks always looked back on these two centuries as their classical age, when their genius had shone at its brightest.

The Greeks remained powerful and creative for another 200 years or more, but gradually the east was lost to them, and the remainder of their world eventually fell under the political dominion of Rome. Nevertheless they kept their language and their intellectual independence. They provided Rome, to a large degree, with its professional classes. Doctors and artists were nearly all Greek. Greeks predominated in education, in engineering, and in the more technical posts in government administration. And in the end the Greeks outlasted their conquerors. When the western Roman Empire disintegrated in the fifth century AD, the eastern, Greek, half continued for another 1,000 years with Constantinople, the former city of

TABLE 1   THE MAIN PERIODS OF GREEK HISTORY

NEOLITHIC	7000–3000 BC	Introduction of settled agriculture
BRONZE AGE	3000–1100 BC	Minoan palaces in Crete, 2000–1450 BC. Fortified centres at Mycenae and elsewhere on the Greek mainland, 1600–1100 BC
DARK AGE	1100–8th cent BC	Protogeometric pottery in Athens from 1050 BC. Geometric pottery in Athens from 900 BC. Settlement or resettlement of sites on Asia Minor coast
ARCHAIC	8th cent– 500 BC	Rise of the city-states. Colonisation in the west and the north
CLASSICAL	500–323 BC	Repulse of the Persian invasions (battles of Marathon, 490 BC; Thermopylae and Salamis, 480 BC; Plataea, 479 BC). Peloponnesian War between Athens and Sparta and their allies, 431–404 BC. Conquest of the Persian empire by Alexander the Great of Macedon, and his death in Babylon in 323 BC
HELLENISTIC	323–30 BC	Division of Alexander's empire into separate kingdoms with their capitals at Pella (Macedonia), Pergamum (Asia Minor), Antioch (Syria), Balkh (Bactria), and Alexandria (Egypt). Expanding dominion of Rome (over S Italy and Sicily by 211 BC; Macedon, mainland Greece, and Pergamum during the 2nd cent; Syria in 64 BC; Rhodes in 43 BC; and Egypt in 30BC)
ROMAN	30 BC–AD 330	
BYZANTINE	AD 330–1453	
TURKISH	AD 1453–1821	
MODERN GREECE	AD 1830 to now	

Byzantium, as its capital. The Byzantine Empire, as it is called, only came to an end in 1453, when Constantinople fell to the Turks. The Greeks were under Turkish rule for nearly 400 years, but their national consciousness and their language survived the ordeal. At last in 1821 came a successful revolt, and in 1830 an independent kingdom was constituted. This was small to start with, but it was the beginning of the modern Greek state.

2

How the Greek World Grew

Early times

IN very early times hunters and plant-gatherers ranged over the mainland of Greece, and recent excavation in the Franchthi cave overlooking the Gulf of Argos suggests that there may have been a continuity between them and the founders of the Neolithic (New Stone) Age culture, which began in Greece around 7000 BC. This age was marked by the introduction of agriculture (cereals and pulses), herding (mainly sheep and goats), and, by 5000 BC, the manufacture of fired clay pottery vessels. Diet was supplemented by hunting and fishing, and the collection of fruit and nuts. Gold, silver, and copper were known and worked from at least 4000 BC, though cutting tools remained predominantly of stone; for small cutting edges these people used obsidian, a black glass-like volcanic rock found on the Aegean island of Melos. Spinning and weaving were among the known crafts. Neolithic settlement was particularly heavy in Thessaly, where the plains favour the cultivation of cereals, but sites occur elsewhere in Greece and not only on the mainland. There was already a village at Knossos in Crete in pre-pottery times, dated by the Carbon 14 method to the end of the seventh millennium: Knossos can claim to be the oldest continuously inhabited site in Europe, and one of the oldest in the world.

The Early Bronze Age in Greece began about 3000 BC. Agriculturally the main innovation was the growing of olive trees and vines. In metallurgy the smelting and casting of bronze (copper alloyed with tin or with arsenic) were introduced, and articles made from bronze came to include axes, daggers, swords, spearheads, saws, chisels, awls, needles, pins, knives, fish-hooks, punches, tweezers. Jewellery and plate might be made of gold, silver, or bronze. In transport, the donkey (whether as a pack animal or for pulling carts or both is still uncertain) and long-oared ships (perhaps 65ft from stem to stern) are both attested for the first time. Sealstones bear witness to the engraver's art and to the property owner's caution. The slow wheel or turntable was known as an aid to the potter, and at the end of this period or the beginning of the next the fast wheel was introduced. Prosperity, to judge from the number and size of known settlements and the high quality of excavated artefacts, seems to have increased steadily, and different cultures can be recognised in the islands (Cycladic), on the mainland (Helladic), and in Crete (Minoan). It is not possible, however, to say who the inhabitants of any of these regions were, or whether they spoke Greek or any language related to it.

The Minoans

The Middle (2200–1500 BC) and the Late (1500–1100 BC) Bronze Age are characterised by the growth of population centres that deserve the name of cities, and by the building of great palaces. Minoan Crete led the way. The palace of Knossos covers some 3 acres of ground, including courtyards, and had an average elevation of two or three storeys. The palaces at Phaistos, Mallia, and Zakro were of comparable dimensions. Minoan palaces existed in smaller towns like Gournia, and a number of sizeable country houses have also been discovered and excavated.

The palaces seem to have played a central part in both the religious and the economic life of Minoan Crete. They contained shrines clearly furnished for ritual use. Bulk granaries were attached to them, and it has been estimated that their store-rooms were able to hold as much as 100,000 litres of oil or wine. It is evident that the palaces also promoted workmanship of high quality. Minoan art, delicate, detailed, and equally successful on the small scale and on the large, can claim to rank among the major art-styles of the world (see plate, p 49).

The period of the palaces saw some important new introductions into the Aegean region. One was sail, which now appears for the first time on representations of ships. Another was the horse, and with it the wheeled vehicle, both chariot and cart. A third, perhaps the most important, was writing. There were two types of writing used in the Minoan palaces – a scantily attested script, generally and misleadingly labelled 'pictographic', and a more amply attested one, called 'Linear A'. Since nothing in Crete during the third millennium foreshadows either script, it looks as if they cannot have been internally developed but must have been brought in from abroad (most likely from Anatolia or the Levant coast) as complete systems of writing, either by immigration or by cultural borrowing. Though the operation of both scripts is probably the same in principle, over half the signs look quite different (as they do, say, in printed English and printed Russian). It is natural to guess that the two scripts were used to write different languages, but we cannot be sure, as we cannot yet read either of them. Most of the inscriptions so far discovered have been on small clay tablets and clay sealings, but there are some on other objects ranging from signet rings and storage jars to small stone altar tables. All of them seem to be classifiable under two heads – account-keeping and religious dedication. Moreover writing seems to have been intimately linked with the palaces. It first appeared with them, and with them it eventually died. The reason may be that it was only ever known and used by palace-trained scribes.

Minoan culture seems to have been remarkably homogeneous throughout Crete. It also extended, either by cultural diffusion or by actual settlement, to the neighbouring islands of Cythera, Melos, Kea, Thera (where dramatic discoveries are

B

now being made), and Rhodes, to Miletus on the mainland of Asia Minor, and beyond Sicily to the Aeolian Islands in the west. The southern part of the Greek mainland, especially Messenia and the Argolid, was also strongly penetrated by Minoan influence.

The end of this brilliant period of Cretan civilisation came suddenly in the middle of the fifteenth century BC, when the archaeological record tells us of widespread fire and destruction throughout the Minoan world. The cause is uncertain. One theory in vogue is that it was an immediate and dramatic result of the Krakatoa-like explosion of the volcanic island Thera in the central Aegean some 50 miles north of central Crete. The other, less romantic, is that the destruction took place some 50 years after the eruption and was the work of foreign invaders from the Greek mainland. Whichever of these explanations is correct, it is certain that in the following period mainland Greeks occupied Knossos and Khania (in the north-west of Crete) and dominated the rest of the island.

The Mycenaeans

The mainland civilisation of this period is generally called Mycenaean after one of its main centres, Mycenae. Artistically and technologically the Mycenaeans had been very much the pupils of Minoan Crete, and now they became its heirs. On the Levant coast, in Egypt, in south Italy and Sicily, we find Mycenaean traders establishing themselves on the sites of former Minoan trading posts. There was also Mycenaean colonisation, both in the west, as at Scoglio del Tonno near Taranto, and more particularly in the east, where there are some fifteen cities on the Asia Minor coast and the neighbouring islands that can plausibly claim Mycenaean ancestry.

Among the crafts the Mycenaeans took over from the Minoan civilisation was that of writing. Thanks to this we think we know who they were, for their account tablets (and they do not seem to have used writing for any purpose other than account-keeping) have been found at Mycenae, Thebes and

Pylos on the mainland and at Knossos and Khania in Crete. The script, known as 'Linear B', has been deciphered (by Michael Ventris in 1953) and shown to have been used for writing Greek. Unfortunately the tablets are purely administrative or accounting records. They give no historical information about the Mycenaean Greeks' arrival in Greece.

The tablets were of unfired clay, and survived because they were baked in the fires that destroyed the buildings; for despite its artistic standards, its partial literacy, and its colonial and mercantile expansion, the Mycenaean age was a time of wars and the destruction of cities. Knossos and Thebes were destroyed early in the period, Pylos and Mycenae itself towards its end, and many others in between, despite the massive walls with which the citadels were generally surrounded. Only Athens, according to tradition, escaped final violence.

The period of Mycenaean glory lasted from about 1500 BC to 1200 BC. It was followed by contraction and decline.

THE DARK AGE

The extent of the decline

The Dark Age, as the name given to it implies, is little known. The most striking fact about it is the tremendous reduction in the number of recognised settlements. We can trace about 320 occupied Mycenaean sites of the thirteenth century BC on the Greek mainland, the islands in the Aegean (excluding Crete) and Ionian Seas, and on the west coast of Asia Minor, but for the twelfth century this number drops to about 130, and for the tenth to about forty. These figures are only approximate, since they are founded on surface observation, and they tell us nothing about the size of the settlements or the density of their occupation. Nevertheless such a heavy reduction in the number of observed sites must imply that there was a great fall in population.

There was certainly a great fall in standards. Among the crafts which either declined seriously or disappeared altogether were those of the scribe, the goldsmith, the silversmith, the worker in ivory, the mason and stonecutter, and in some areas the bronze-worker – in short all the arts that had been necessary for the previous palace civilisation.

It is not yet possible to link the known facts of the period into a connected history. To begin with, we do not know who or what was responsible for the destruction of the Mycenaean palaces. Foreign invaders, passing raiders, revolutions, dynastic wars between the cities, have all been proposed. So has a change in the direction of the prevailing winds, leading to a catastrophic drought in most of the main areas of Mycenaean settlement. Whatever the cause, the destructions themselves and the subsequent drop in population must have made it an extremely unpleasant time to live through. As for the next 400 years, we remain very much in the dark. Quite a number of cemeteries are known, but few settlement sites, and there is little memory of the period in Greek tradition to give name or meaning to the archaeological discoveries. It does not amount to more than a few genealogies and a few accounts of population movement.

It is perhaps possible to detect two types of community. Mycenaeans of the old culture seem to have survived for a time, and not only in their old homes. Mycenaean émigrés went to Cyprus in the twelfth century BC, and to Achaea in the north-west Peloponnese, an area where the population in the Dark Age may have actually risen. On the other hand there are traces of communities which, though Mycenaean enough in many respects, such as their pottery, followed some decidedly different customs. Long dress-pins, found in the graves of their womenfolk, had obviously been used for fastening garments at the shoulder in a quite un-Mycenaean fashion. The *fibula*, or safety-pin, was much more widely used. Their graves were not multiple graves such as the Mycenaeans had favoured, but single ones, and were often dug inside earlier Mycenaean settlement areas. The identity of these people is still uncertain. If they were newcomers, they can perhaps be identified with the ancestors of the Dorians of classical times. But the differences between them and the adherents of the old Mycenaean customs are really very slight. They need not have moved in. They may have just moved with the times.

For the times did move. Despite the impoverishment and isolation there was one major innovation. This was iron-working. The technology seems to have reached Greece from North Syria via Cyprus about 1050 BC. At this stage iron probably had no advantages over bronze, not even for hardness of cutting edge, but it was available when bronze was not, and ultimately it was to become far more plentiful. There was also one minor innovation of the same date. It was found that the multiple brush, a device which had been known for a very long time, could be attached to a compass and used for tracing concentric circles. This discovery, which was apparently made in Athens and helped in the development there of a new pottery style known to us as Protogeometric, was trivial enough in itself, but it shows that the Dark Age was not so dark that there was a total eclipse of human ingenuity.

The question of continuity

One of the most interesting questions about the Dark Age is how far the lines were kept open between the high points of Bronze Age and Classical Greek civilisation. In Crete there was certainly a strong measure of continuity. Minoan traditions in building, pottery, and above all in religious practices continued not only in ancient centres like Knossos but in quite new ones like the mountain village or refuge of Karphi, which only dates from about 1150 BC. Elsewhere there are often gaps. Delos and Delphi, two great religious sanctuaries of classical times, both seem to have been Mycenaean cult-centres too, but on both sites there is only scanty Dark Age pottery, not enough to prove uninterrupted use. At Amyclae in the southern Peloponnese there is a clear gap of 100 years between the latest Mycenaean pottery found in the sanctuary area and the earliest protogeometric; but Hyacinthus was worshipped there in classical times, and Hyacinthus is a name of pre-Greek type.

So continuity seems certain despite the archaeological gap. There is a similar puzzle in respect of places in the eastern Aegean. Many sites (at Smyrna, Erythrae, Ephesus, Miletus; in the Dodecanese; and on the south-west Asia Minor coast) were occupied in the tenth century, and many others (at Colophon, Clazomenae, Phocaea, Samos, and on the island of Chios) in the ninth or eighth century BC; and most, perhaps all, of them had been previously occupied by Mycenaeans. In the intervening period, however, many seem to have been deserted. Was it a coincidence that the same sites were resettled? If it was not a coincidence, how were they remembered? Again, there is a tomb on the island of Cos in the Dodecanese which contained protogeometric pottery and must therefore belong to the tenth century BC; but it also contained some Mycenaean pottery, including a fine vase of the fourteenth century. Was this vase accidentally discovered in an ancient grave by the Dark Age inhabitants of Cos, or was it an heirloom? There was a temple at Ayia Irini on the island of Keos off the tip of Attica which was built in the fifteenth century BC and was still in use in the fifth century BC, when it was a shrine of Dionysus. Was the tradition of worship continuous? Unfortunately different rooms were used at different times, so we cannot be sure.

Nevertheless many important things certainly did survive without break – the cultivation of the olive and the vine, traditions of pottery manufacture, the memory of people and places in heroic story, religious myths and observances (many of them attached to old Mycenaean centres), and above all the Greek language itself. So the great surge of new enterprise which began in the eighth century BC should probably be seen as a renaissance rather than as a rise from nothing. There was nostalgia as well as progress. Above all, it was the golden age of Homeric poetry, and the Homeric bards were busy exploring the past at the same time as the navigators and colonists were founding the future.

THE GREAT EXPANSION

Greece at the end of the Dark Age

The Greek world of 776 BC – the date of the founding of the Olympic Games and the date that has always been conventionally taken as the beginning of Greek history – consisted of the island of Crete in the south, the islands of the Aegean northwards as far as the fortieth parallel, the coast of Asia Minor to the east, and the mainland of southern Greece across to the Ionian islands in the west. Beyond these limits were the barbarians, as the Greeks called all those who were not Greek, irrespective of their cultural status. The peoples of southern Italy and Sicily, the Illyrians and Thracians in the Balkan peninsula to their north, and some of the peoples of Asia Minor were more backward than the Greeks. Others in Asia Minor, like the Lydians, were perhaps more advanced. A little further away were the direct heirs of the Bronze Age civilisations of the Near East – the Phoenicians on the Levant coast, the Assyrians beyond them in northern Mesopotamia, and the Egyptians in the valley of the Nile. The Etruscans, whose origin is still unknown but who probably came from Asia Minor, were at the time beginning to establish themselves in central Italy.

Colonisation 776–600 BC

This small Greek world was to expand prodigiously during the next two centuries until it encircled almost the whole of the Mediterranean and the Black Sea. The expansion was effected piecemeal by the sending out of colonies from many different cities (see Table 2, pp 27–8) and for many different reasons. One obvious reason was trade. Al Mina in Syria, Naucratis in Egypt, Pithecoussae on the island of Ischia (concerned with north Italian iron), Massalia (Marseille) at the mouth of the Rhône (on a tin route), and Emporion (Ampurias, the Greek name meaning 'market') in north Spain, are examples. Other colonies seem to have been founded to guard a trade-route, such as Zancle (Messina) and Rhegium (Reggio di Calabria).

Another motive for colonisation could be land-hunger caused by overpopulation at home. This seems to have been the reason for Thera's colonisation of Cyrene. There were cases of *force majeure*. The Eretrians, who originally founded Corcyra (Corfu), are said to have been evicted by the Corinthians, and to have gone off and founded Methone in the Gulf of Salonika. Less typical was the case of Taras (Taranto), a Spartan colony. The original colonists were bastards, or so the story goes. During a particularly long military campaign, with most husbands away from home, Sparta had found it necessary to take emergency measures to maintain the population. The measures were successful, but when matters returned to normal at the end of the war, civic liabilities were imposed on the irregularly conceived offspring. Not unnaturally, it is said, they resented this, and emigrated to found Taras.

We have no historical account of the founding of an early colony, but in the *Odyssey* Homer tells us how the Phaeacians came to settle in the imaginary land of Scheria:

> *The Phaeacians had once lived in the broad land of Hyperia. But their neighbours, the Cyclopes, were overbearing, continually troublesome, and superior in the field. So their king Nausithous* [*the name means 'Swift-shipped'*] *made them move and settle in Scheria, far away from human greed. He drove a wall round the city, built houses and temples, and apportioned the land into fields. In the course of time he had died and gone to Hades, and now Alcinous* ['*Valiant-of-Mind'*] *was their ruler . . .*

Homer's Phaeacians moved as a whole community. More usual was colonisation proper, when a mother-city sent out some of its members. We know something about the procedure. It was customary to have an official founder. He was not necessarily a man of any great consequence during his lifetime in his mother-city, but naturally enough he would become an important figure in the memory of future generations in the colony, and might even come to be venerated in official cult as a semi-divine hero. When a colony founded another colony, as often happened, the founder was normally chosen from the grandmother-city.

In arranging the future of a colony one of the most important and universal provisions was for equality of treatment for all colonists, both in legal status and in the initial distribution of land. The colonists did not usually have an automatic right to return to their native city. In fact, if the reason for the foundation was to relieve overpopulation at home, return might be made very difficult. In other cases return might be permitted, provided that the returning colonist left behind him an adult male of his family – clearly in order to protect the future welfare of the colony. In the matter of free movement the citizens of the mother-city tended to be given preferential treatment. They frequently had the right to go and live in the colony at any future date, and even to take precedence on social and religious occasions in the colony should they be visiting it.

The colonies' relations with the local populations varied. We hear of Greek colonists evicting inhabitants by force, but also of Greek colonists being invited to settle. A Greek colony might well benefit the region in which it established itself, raising the standard of living and bringing international contact. Where more advanced civilisations already existed, as on the Levant coast, in Egypt, in Etruria, and later in the Carthaginian sphere of influence, Greek colonies were either not planted or operated under special conditions, like Naucratis, whose position as a licensed Greek colony in Egypt must have been very like the position of Shanghai as a European trading post in China before World War II.

Colonisation was not universally successful. Colonies were planted in the Balearics, on the south coast of Spain, in Corsica, perhaps in Sardinia, and perhaps on the Tunis coast, but they were all lost before the end of the sixth century, partly to the Etruscans, but mainly to the Carthaginians. Mostly though, the colonies thrived, sometimes becoming richer than their mother-cities, and Greek influence spread far inland from them. The tomb of a Celtic princess at Vix on the Seine 100 miles above Paris contained Athenian cups and a bronze vase, probably from Sparta, of large size and fine workmanship. Another bronze vase of Spartan manufacture and early sixth-century date has been found at Grächwyl in Switzerland. At Vettersfelde not far from Berlin a Scythian chief was buried with his personal arms and his horse's equipment decorated with the work of Ionian Greek craftsmen. He had presumably commissioned them at one of Miletus's colonies on the Black Sea. When King Darius of Persia built his new palace at Persepolis, he employed Greek masons and Greek artists. Greek mercenary soldiers were employed in Egypt in both the seventh and the sixth centuries BC; they even reached, and defaced with their signatures, the great statues of Rameses at Abu Simbel.

Thus the Greeks, a far from numerous people even by the standards of those times, had made their presence felt over a very wide area of the world while they were still in their archaic age, before the pattern of their civilisation had settled into its definitive form. What we now consider most characteristic of ancient Greece – the temples flanked with great marble columns, the lifelike statues, the machinery of democracy, drama, philosophy, history, science, and medicine – was only just emerging or lay still hidden in the future.

Greatest extent of the Greek world

Greek colonisation did not stop in 600 BC. Far from it. But after this it became, for the most part what town-planners call in-filling, ie new colonies were planted on already colonised coastlines, but no new areas (except in the Adriatic) were opened up for settlement in the next two and a half centuries. The Greek world seemed to have reached its geographical limits, and that might have been so, if it had not been for the Persian Empire.

That Empire was created in an astonishing 25 years during which the four major powers of the time were conquered and their territory annexed by Cyrus and his son Cambyses. Media fell in 549, Lydia in 546, Babylon in 538, and Egypt in 525 BC. These conquests, equivalent in scale and speed to those of the

TABLE 2   EARLY GREEK COLONISATION

Location	Approximate date of first settlement	Name of colony	Mother-city
WEST			
Ischia	before 760	Pithecoussae	Eretria and Chalcis
Corfu	before 733	Corcyra	Eretria
Campania	750	Cumae	Chalcis
nr Taormina	734	Naxos	Chalcis
Lentini	729	Leontini	Chalcis
Catania	729	Catane	Chalcis
Messina	730	Zancle	Chalcis
Milazzo	716	Mylae	Chalcis
Reggio	725	Rhegium	Chalcis and Messenians from S Peloponnese
Syracuse	733	Syracuse	Corinth
Corfu	refounded 733	Corcyra	Corinth
nr Augusta	728	Megara Hyblaea	Megara
Gulf of Taranto	720	Sybaris	Achaeans from NW Peloponnese
Crotone	708	Croton	Achaeans
Metaponto	700	Metapontium	Achaeans
Taranto	705	Taras	Sparta
Gulf of Salerno	700	Posidonia	Sybaris (?)
Gela	688	Gela	Rhodians and Cretans
Locri	673	Locri	Locris
Gulf of Taranto	650	Siris	Colophon
SE Calabria	660	Caulonia	Croton
inland of Syracuse	663	Acrae	Syracuse
Monte Casale (?)	643	Casmenae	Syracuse
nr Vittoria	598	Camarina	Syracuse
SW Sicily	by 628	Selinus	Megara Hyblaea
Marseilles	600	Massalia	Phocaea
Ampurias	600	Emporion	Phocaea
Balearic Islands	654	?	Rhodians
Durazzo	627	Epidamnus	Corcyra
NORTH			
Kassandra peninsula SW of Salonica	8th	Mende	Eretria

Location	Approximate date of first settlement	Name of colony	Mother-city
Kassandra peninsula	8th	Scione	Eretria
Gulf of Thermae S of Salonica	733	Methone	Eretria
Island of Thasos	685	Thasos	Paros
Kavalla	after 685	Neapolis	Thasos
Avdira (nr Porto Lago)	650	Abdera	Clazomenae
Maronia	7th	Maronia	Chios
Erdek peninsula (Sea of Marmora)	7th	Cyzicus	Miletus
Dardanelles	late 7th	Abydos	Miletus
Dardanelles	7th	Sigeum	Aeolians
Istanbul	7th	Byzantium	Megara
nr Sozopol	7th	Apollonia	Miletus
S of Danube	7th	Istros	Miletus
mouth of Bug	7th	Olbia	Miletus
Crimea (Kerch)	7th	Panticapaeum	Miletus
SOUTH			
Egypt (nr Sais)	7th	Naucratis	Miletus and other Ionian cities
Lybia	630	Cyrene	Thera

Arabs after Mohammed, made Persia the heir of all the major
Bronze Age civilisations of the Near East, and the master of the
largest empire the world had yet seen. Included in it since 545
BC had been the Greek cities of the Asia Minor coast, but their
desire for independence had been naturally kept alive by the
existence of the free Greek cities across the water, and eventually Persia decided to incorporate these too. A preliminary
expedition, mounted by Darius, was defeated by the Athenians
at Marathon in 490 BC. Ten years later a much larger force
under the personal command of the king, Xerxes, crossed the
Bosporus to carry out the annexation. The campaign, which
included the celebrated battles of Thermopylae, Salamis, and
Plataea, was always regarded by the later Greeks as their most

glorious moment of achievement and as a major turning point in their history. Its immediate result was the total defeat of the invading army. Its long-term effect was to put the hope of revenge and conquest of Persia as a plausible item on the pro-gramme of panhellenic (all-Greek) nationalism. The crusade was not to come for 150 years, but when it did, its success was complete.

Alexander of Macedon – Macedon was now the ruling state in Greece – launched his attack on the Persian Empire in 334 BC. During the next ten years he not only defeated the numeri-cally far superior Persian army, but annexed and reorganised the whole of the former Persian empire from Egypt to Afghani-stan, and entered India itself. There his troops mutinied and forced him to turn back. But though he died of a fever at Babylon in the next year (323 BC), and though his successors quarrelled and divided his empire into separate kingdoms which continued to quarrel with each other for the best part of the next 300 years, the result of his victories was a massive and enduring extension of the Greek world.

Egypt, Syria, and Asia Minor became half Greek, and their great capital cities of Alexandria, Antioch, and Pergamum became major centres of learning and commerce. Further east there was a separate Greek kingdom established in Bactria, then no desert but rich prairie land at an important cross-route of trade. Greek kings ruled in Afghanistan, where Kanda-har, founded by Alexander, still perpetuates his name. They even ruled in the Punjab, the most famous of them being Menander (c180–130 BC), whose memory is still revered by Buddhists as far afield as Ceylon, Burma, and Thailand.

The reign of the last of the Greek kings in India, Hermaeus, came to an end soon after the middle of the first century BC, but the Greek language and aspects of the Greek way of life per-sisted for a century longer, and a few Greek words (eg for pen and ink and for bridle) even found their way into Sanskrit. At the southern tip of India Greek janissaries guarded the palace and patrolled the streets of Madura after dark (armed with whips, swords, and drink according to the Tamil poet who

tells us of them), and their were prosperous Greek quarters in
the trading cities on the Malabar and Coromandel coasts in
the first century AD. 'The beautifully-built ships of the Yavanas
[Greeks] come with gold and return with pepper', said a local
poet, and a Greek navigator's manual, the *Periplus* of the Red
Sea, confirms these as the main items of trade, though it adds
others. Some idea of the scale of the trade is given by the Greek
geographer Strabo, who was in Egypt in 24 BC and tells us that
120 merchantmen a year sailed to India from Myos-Hormos.
They made the voyage direct in both directions, using the
monsoon or 'wind of Hippalus', as they called it after its Greek
discoverer Hippalus, who probably lived in the first century BC.

Greek India was an exotic and remote corner of Greek civilisation. Its impact was great at the time in fields as diverse as
stone building, sculpture, military and hydraulic engineering,
coinage, metallurgy, medicine, and astronomy, but it is difficult to prove that it left to India any legacy of lasting historical
importance. In one respect, though, it may serve to correct our
historical perspectives. In Europe the Greeks have often been
regarded, in contrast to their Roman successors, as people
whose gifts lay in the domain of theory, in poetry, philosophy,
pure science, and fine art; but the detached and distant witness
of ancient India shows them in quite a different light. The
stereotype of the Greek in Tamil poetry is that of the man of
war, the man of money, and the man of technical know-how.

3

Who the Greeks Were

... the common factors of our Greekness, blood, language, the sanctuaries of the gods and their sacrifices, the same way of life ...

Herodotus, viii, 144 (c430 BC)

RACE

THE ancient Greek historian Herodotus listed race as one of four factors making for national identity. Intellectual fashion of a century ago thought it even more important than that. 'All is race; there is no other truth', argued a character in *Tancred*, one of Disraeli's political novels, and Disraeli let him win the argument. Historians of the late nineteenth and early twentieth centuries tried hard to identify the racial character of the Greeks and came to the conclusion that they were in origin blonde blue-eyed Aryans, though subsequently corrupted by the intermixture of Mediterranean and other stock. Today the concept of race, largely owing to its misuse by politicians, is out of fashion, and we read that the ancient Greeks, like their modern successors, were of all sorts, with their hair ranging from blonde to black and their eyes from blue to brown, and their skulls of assorted sizes and shapes. Doubtless this picture is very much nearer the truth. Nevertheless it remains true that though the ancient Greeks may not have been Nordic, they were not Negroid or Mongolian either. It is clear that race must mean something. The trouble is that we do not

31

know exactly what. More than that we do not even know how to recognise it in an ancient culture. Technology, style of dress, burial customs, religious belief – none of these are necessarily related to race, as a moment's consideration of the modern world will show. Nor is language – we need think only of the diffusion of Arabic in the first millennium AD or of English in the last 100 years. So until more precise information becomes available (as it may do through the study of genetics), we shall do best to leave aside all guesswork about the racial constitution of the ancient Greeks and the contribution it may have made to the flowering of their civilisation.

LANGUAGE

By origin Greek is an Indo-European language, like Sanskrit, Persian, Russian, German, Latin, and many other languages, including English. What this means is that the basic grammatical concepts revealed by these languages and much of their vocabulary for common objects and experiences can be shown to have descended from the same source. Unfortunately it is not yet known where this source was or when it broke up. Nor, even if it were known, would the statement that Greek is an Indo-European language help us to understand the Greeks any more than the equally true statement that English is a Germanic language helps us to understand Britain or the United States of America.

However, we may learn something if we can isolate the alien elements. For instance, English has a great number of words, mainly from French, Latin, and Greek, superimposed on its Anglo-Saxon foundations. The observation that the basic words tend to relate to basic needs and to production while the foreign ones relate to enjoyment and to scientific inquiry (thus we breed *sheep*, eat *mutton*, and classify the bones as *ovine* if we want to be *technical* about it) gives us some insight into English social history. We find something similar with the vocabulary of Greek. About a third of it cannot be explained as Indo-

European. Most of the alien words relate to luxury articles, to crops that are particularly at home in the Mediterranean, to religion, and to trade. A sample list shows clearly the sort of more advanced culture that seems to have been superimposed on the original foundations: *chrysos*, gold; *kassiteros*, tin; *asaminthos*, bath; *chiton*, tunic; *apēnē*, chariot; *sagēnē*, seine-net; *elai(w)a*, olive; *(w)oinos*, wine; *sykon*, fig; *terebinthos*, turpentine; *narkissos*, narcissus; *kolossos*, votive statue; *bretas*, a religious statue made of wood; *Athene, Artemis, Apollo*, names of gods; *sakkos*, sack; *kados*, jar; and *mna*, unit of weight.

The first two words of this list may be Hurrian, and the last two are Semitic. Most are of unknown origin, but are sometimes classified as 'Aegean' or 'Mediterranean' on the ground that they include words for Mediterranean flora of the same pattern as Mediterranean place-names (for instance, *Halikarnassos* and *kyparissos*, cypress; *Korinthos* and *terebinthos*, terebinth, turpentine).

This massive importation of words into Greek seems to have taken place before the end of the Bronze Age, but we cannot say how long before or how many different sources contributed. If words are the vehicle of civilisation, however, this enrichment of the vocabulary must have played a significant part in preparing the ground for the later creativity of the Greek people.

In classical times there were numerous local Greek dialects, which are known to us mainly from inscriptions. The major dialects, canonised as such by their use in literature, were Aeolic, Ionic, Attic (the form of Ionic spoken in Athens), and Doric. Eventually Attic triumphed because of the cultural predominance of Athens, and the *koinê*, the common Greek developed in the Hellenistic Age, was derived from it. The *koinê* in its turn is the ancestor of modern Greek.

The early history of the dialects is still subject to dispute. It would seem that they can be classified into two main groups, East Greek and West Greek. Ionic and the Greek of the Mycenaean Linear B tablets, belong to the former, Doric to the latter. Before this there must have been a period of common

C

Greek, since all the dialects share a number of features that distinguish Greek from other Indo-European languages, but it is not known when or where this common Greek was spoken.

COMMON TRADITIONS

Religion

Ancient Greek religion is as all-pervasive and as hard to define as the odour of incense that rose from the altars in the smiling countryside through which the soul travelled on its way to heaven, according to the poet Pindar. There did exist religion of the type we are used to, characterised by an admission ceremony, doctrine, rules of conduct, and the promise of personal salvation. In fact there were several such religions, some from the east, and they became increasingly fashionable in Hellenistic and Roman times. The earliest of them, dating from well before the classical period, was Greek – the Mysteries of the two goddesses, Demeter and her daughter Persephone, at Eleusis near Athens. When Athens annexed Eleusis shortly before 600 BC, the Mysteries were put under official Athenian supervision. There was an annual procession for initiates in the autumn, followed by a service or ceremony at which songs were sung, rites were performed, and objects were displayed. But the details were secret and the secret was kept. It is probable that the myth of the rape of Persephone was told or enacted at some stage, possible that the supreme mystery shown was an ear of corn, and pretty certain that one comfort the initiates derived from it all was the hope of immortality.

The hallmark of these mystery religions was the revelation of a secret truth. The more normal form of Greek religion was public. Here the important distinction was not between true and false or between good and evil but between the known and the unknown. Everything outside human control or understanding was a god or the manifestation of a god. The scope was therefore very wide indeed.

At the most personal level were the bonds that held society

together. Every family had an altar to Zeus in the courtyard
of its house, and numerous customs and ceremonies of daily
life, each of which had a deity associated with it. Beyond the
immediate family each clan or tribe had its cult centres, its
festivals and sacrifices, and a hero or god from whom it traced
its descent. At the top of this particular ladder came the god or
gods of the city.

Quite different in function from these gods of society were the
gods of nature. At the local level there were numerous gods or
spirits of particular caves, springs, woods, and rivers. More
general concepts like Dawn and the North Wind, phenomena
like fire and earthquakes, and the universal presences of
nature like the sun, moon, sea, and sky, could also be thought
of as deities, for they all possessed in their different ways a life
of their own outside human control.

In yet another category were the gods who inspired a man
with the skills of his trade or profession – the gods of poets,
prostitutes, heralds, musicians, doctors, merchants. Knack is a
mysterious thing, not immediately teachable and easily lost. It
was therefore natural for the Greeks to think of it as god-given.

Needless to say these different functional categories were not
so rigidly compartmentalised in the religious imagination of
the Greeks. One god could play many parts. Athena was both
the city goddess of Athens and a patroness of craftsmanship.
Apollo was strongly associated with particular sanctuaries,
Delphi and Delos being the most important, but could also be
identified with the sun, and was also the patron of music. The
more of these pluralities a god held, the higher his prestige,
particularly of course if he figured in Homer. But however
famous a god or goddess might become, the particular cults
always remained local. Athena and Apollo were known
throughout the Greek world, but there was never a Chief
Priestess of Athena or a Chief Priest of Apollo with overriding
powers, only the priest or priestess of a particular temple or
sanctuary. Their appointments were made, and the various
cults, festivals, and sacrifices were organised, by the communities – family, tribe, city, or other association – which

owned the temple or were most directly concerned with it. What the individual worshipper received in return for his prayers and his participation was the comfort of having propitiated as far as he could a power which, unpropitiated, might do him harm, and a sense of belonging to the community and to its traditions.

Legend and myth

One of the strongest links between Greeks was a common fund of story. Some of it was historical in essence, about real places and real people, though often romanticised almost beyond recognition. True history, in the sense of events being recorded by contemporaries in a permanent form that could be verified by future generations, did not exist much, if at all, before the Persian Wars (490–479 BC). When we try to look back beyond them, the view becomes misty. The politicians of the sixth century are remembered for isolated facts and isolated pronouncements rather than for coherent lives. A century further back and even the founders of colonies are either not remembered at all, or, if they are, have their lives so wrapped in oracles, portents, and romance that reality is indiscernible.

Another step into the past and we are with the heroes of the Trojan War, who walked with the gods and who could hurl stones that no two men of today could even lift. Before them was an even more supernatural world – that of the Argonauts and their miracle-filled voyage to recover the Golden Fleece from its guardian dragon, of Theseus and the Minotaur, of Heracles and his Twelve Labours, of Perseus rescuing Andromeda. Nevertheless all these people, even the last, were thought of as in some sense real. Their names and stories are attached to historical Greek cities, and except for the fact that their ultimate ancestor, being unknown, is usually said to be a god, they were given historically plausible family trees.

The other main category of Greek story had a different aim. It did not tell of past glories but explained things as they were in the present. Such was the story that told how Heaven and

Earth had come into being, and how Heaven was replaced first
by Kronos and then by the present ruler of the gods, Zeus.
Another related how Prometheus annoyed his cousin Zeus by
giving mankind the use of fire, a secret previously known only
in heaven, and how Zeus took a terrible revenge on mankind
by creating for them a torture they could neither live with nor
live without – woman. A third recounted the tale of Deucalion
and Pyrrha, the son and niece of Prometheus, who refounded
the human race after it had been wiped out by Zeus in a flood.
These myths are evidently set on a different plane of reality
from the other kind. Some of them, indeed, are not Greek in
origin, the one about the succession of the gods and the one
about the flood coming originally from Babylon.

Stories of both classes were transmitted by epic poetry. The
earliest epic poets, or rather the earliest whose names are preserved and to whom definite works are attributed, were Homer
and Hesiod. The image of the heroic world and of heroic
virtues, which every Greek carried in his mind and which he
often enough strove to imitate in his actions, was created by
Homer, who for this reason, if for no other, was the more
important of the two.

Festivals and games

Religious festivals and games enjoyed a supra-national status
within the Greek world, being the only institutional bond that
existed between all Greek speakers regardless of city. Hesiod
tells us that he competed for a poetry prize at the funeral games
of a local prince called Amphidamas in Euboea, and won a
bronze tripod. The date would have been about 700 BC or soon
after. Such festivals were the milieu in which epic poetry was
created and preserved during the next two or three hundred
years. In a dialogue by Plato we have a vivid glimpse of the life
of a rhapsode (a professional reciter) called Ion, who made his
living by reciting Homer at panhellenic festivals. Socrates
questions him:

'*Where have you come from? From your home town, Ephesus?*'
'*No, from Epidaurus. From the Festival of Asclepius.*'
'*I never knew his ritual included competitions in reciting.*'
'*It does, and all the other usual poetic and musical events.*'
'*So you competed. You were successful, I hope.*'
'*First prize.*'
'*Splendid! And you have now come to Athens to win another victory in the Panathenaic Games?*'
'*Yes, God willing.*'

Later Ion describes the atmosphere of his recitations:

'*To be honest with you, Socrates, I must admit that when I come to a sad part, my own eyes fill with tears, when there are horrors or thrills, my hair stands on end and my heart jumps . . . I look down from my platform and can see them tearful or horror-struck in the grip of my narrative. My livelihood depends on it. If I can make them cry their money cheers me up. But if they laugh, I can cry and cry for all the good it will do me.*'

Older and more famous than the Festival of Asclepius at Epidaurus, and more international than the Panathenaic Festival at Athens, were the four great Panhellenic Games. The Isthmian (near Corinth) and the Nemean (at Nemea in the northern Peloponnese) were held every two years, and the Pythian (at Delphi) and the Olympic (on the River Alpheus in the western Peloponnese) every four. The Olympic Games were the greatest of all, their foundation in 776 BC coming to be used as the Greeks' historical dating point, as we use the birth of Christ. Their span of life – from 776 BC to AD 392, after which they were banned as pagan by the Christian emperor Theodosius – was co-terminous with ancient Greek civilisation. They were even seen as being a revival of an earlier heroic custom founded by Heracles. 'Out of love for Greece', to quote a speech delivered at the Games of 388 BC by Lysias, a prominent Athenian of the time, 'Heracles created these Games as an opportunity for competitive displays of wealth, physique, and intellect, in one of the most beautiful places in the Greek world, in order to bring us all together with lots to see and lots to listen to in the belief that these reunions of Greeks might be the beginning of peace and understanding among us.'

This was no doubt fanciful history, and most of the programme in Lysias' time dated only from the sixth century BC. Nevertheless what Lysias said was genuine enough as contemporary aspiration. Indeed the Olympic Games were institutionally linked to peace. Visitors to them were given safe conduct, the ground itself was sacred, and, while the festival was on, fighting in any wars that were currently being waged in Greece was suspended.

The keynote of the Games was glory – glory for oneself and glory for one's city. In so far as the two can be separated, the former was brought by victory in the athletic events, especially the foot-race, and the latter by victory in the chariot-race. In this money talked. Equipping a chariot was expensive, and a high proportion of the winners in the event came from the rich colonial cities of southern Italy and Sicily. A victory meant a tremendous fêting on one's return home, but the prize was purely nominal, a garland of olive.

Not only was the glory in the competition, there was glory in the surroundings. The sanctuary of Zeus in which the Games were held was blessed by nature – it stood in a well watered and well wooded valley – and improved by art. Fame had brought prosperity. Marble sparkled from the proud columns of temples and secular buildings, statues of past victors encouraged ambition, and there were unique monuments such as Phidias's gold and ivory statue of Zeus (c430 BC) and the Persian armour from Marathon dedicated by Athens.

Finally there was glory in the people who came. They included the famous and the fashionable, not only athletes and aristocrats but also artists and philosophers. Lysias' remark about the display of intellect at Olympia was confirmed by the German excavations there. A statue to the educationist Gorgias had been erected in Olympia after his death in the first half of the fourth century BC, and the Germans found its pedestal inscribed with a verse epitaph:

Not for great wealth did Gorgias win his place
Of honour in Apollo's muster-roll,
But as a man of modesty and grace
And as an expert trainer of the soul.

Literacy and law

The Greek alphabet was taken over from the Semitic alphabet of north-west Syria, probably in the eighth century BC. It spread through the independent city-states of the Greek world somewhat haphazardly. There was no standard version, and each local script had its own alphabet and its own shapes for the letters (see Fig 2). Our own alphabet descends, through Latin, from one of these early forms. Eventually the Ionian alphabet, though we do not know why, ousted the other local scripts one by one, in much the same way as the metric system has ousted so many local units of measurement in the modern world.

In contrast to the civilisations of the Near East, where writing was confined to those whose profession it was (like driving a train), literacy in Greece was unrestricted and anyone could learn the art and use it (like driving a car). From at least the sixth century BC onwards reading and writing were taught without distinction of sex to those who wanted tuition and could afford it. It is generally assumed in the public institutions of classical times that most people, or at least most people in towns, whether rich, poor, slave, free, male, or female, can read and write, and this impression is confirmed by the casual remarks of contemporary writers. There are of course no figures for literacy rates. One imagines that they varied from place to place, being high in cities, low in isolated areas like Arcadia and in rigidly conservative societies like Sparta and Crete.

Unrestricted literacy meant that there could be a public literature as opposed to an exclusively religious or court literature. This possibility was to be amply fulfilled in later times, though the habit of ordinary individuals possessing and reading books cannot be traced back much before 425 BC. Before that

Greek letter name	North Semitic letter form	Euboea and western colonies	Standard Latin form	Corinth	Early Ionic	Standard Greek form
alpha	ⱪ	Λ	A	Λ	Λ	A
beta	9	B	B	⎍	B	B
gamma	⌐	Γ, ⟨	C, (G)	Γ, ⟨	Γ	Γ
delta	◁	Δ, D	D	Δ	Δ	Δ
epsilon	⊰	Ϝ	E	B, Ϝ	Ϝ	E
vau	Υ	Ϝ	F	F		
zeta	Ⅰ	I	(Z)	I	I	I Z
eta	⍢	Β, H	H, H	Β	Β	H
theta	⊕	⊕		⊕	⊕	θ
iota	⅂	I	I	⟨	I	I
kappa	⅄	K	K	K	K	K
lambda	⎿	Ⳑ	L	Γ	Γ	Λ
mu	ⱳ	M, M	M	⋀	⋀	M
nu	⅄	ᴎ	N	ᴎ	ᴎ	N
xi	ⱦ	X	X	Ⱦ	Ⱦ, Ξ	Ξ
omikron	O	O	O	O	O	O
pi	⅂	Γ	P	Γ	Γ	Π
san	ⱶ	M		M		
qoppa	φ	φ	Q	φ	φ	
rho	⠘	P, R	R	Ρ	Ρ	P
sigma	w	⟩	S	⟨, ⟩	Σ	
tau	ⵜ	T	T	T	T	T
upsilon		ⴼ	V, Y	ⴼ	V, ⴼ	
phi		φ		φ	φ	φ
chi		Ψ, ⱱ		X	X	X
psi				Ψ, ⴽ	Ψ, ⴽ	Ψ
omega					Ω	Ω

The development of the Greek alphabet

the vehicle of communication was the spoken word or the song. Writing was only to record the performance, and (perhaps) to assist the memory of the reciter.

Another effect, and for the archaic period a very much more important effect, of the unrestricted literacy of the Greek cities was political. The written law and the written inventory could be read by all. The private citizen could, and did, argue for his rights, and the public official could be, and frequently was, called to book. The texts of public laws, inventories, and accounts were inscribed on stone and erected where everybody could read them, and the stone inscription counted as the authorised text from which courts and public bodies, like individuals, had to take copies when they needed them. In this way writing was a main bastion of Greek democracy wherever it flourished and perhaps the most important single factor distinguishing the ancient Greeks from all other ancient peoples.

ENVIRONMENT

Mountains and sea

Prehistorians speculate about the Greeks before they reached Greece, and Greek communities at various times in history have maintained themselves in other parts of the world. Nevertheless the Greeks have been in their homeland for so long and have so little succeeded in flourishing outside it that it may almost be considered a part of their identity. Greece is a land of mountains. The highest, Mount Olympus where the gods lived, is 9,550ft, and there are many peaks over 6,000ft. Limestone predominates, and makes for a rugged countryside. The plains, cradled in the mountains or on the coast between the mountains and the sea, are for the most part fairly small and isolated from each other. The coastline itself is much indented with gulfs and inlets so that hardly anywhere in Greece is more than 50 miles from the sea. The islands are numerous and range in size up to the 160 mile-long island of Crete. Over fifty are suitable for habitation – some of them wooded and fertile, others bare and able to yield only the sparest of livings. The coast of Asia Minor, which in classical times was full of Greek cities, has rich alluvial plains, and the Ionians, the main branch of the Greeks settled there, had a reputation for luxury living.

Since Wordsworth wrote his sonnet beginning:

> *Two Voices are there; one is of the sea*
> *One of the mountains; each a mighty Voice,*
> *In both from age to age thou didst rejoice,*
> *They were thy chosen music, Liberty!*

mountains and sea have shared a common pigeonhole with democracy in the minds of English-speaking people, and often enough Greece has been bundled into it too. The Greeks themselves had a rather different attitude. To them 'the shadowy mountains and the echoing sea', as Homer calls them, were what divided communities from each other. In so far as mountains projected a sentimental image, it was not as a nurse of political liberties but as the haunt of wild nature. Artemis, the untamed virgin huntress, the goat-like Pan, and Dionysus in his more violent aspect, were the gods that the Greeks associated with mountains. They talked of mountain-dancing and mountain-madness. In numerous passages of Greek poetry the mountains are seen as offering spiritual escape from the pressures of rational life.

The Greek image of the sea was also different from ours. The note of 'All I ask is a tall ship and a star to steer her by' is absent from Greek literature. Though some romance and exhilaration was evidently felt at Athens in connection with the rowing of naval triremes, travelling by sea was in general looked on as something that had to be done, not as a source of enjoyment. When the poet Sophocles made a list of the unnatural innovations made by man, he headed it with seafaring. Nevertheless the sea was often the only way to get from one Greek city to another, and communities living too far from it tended to stagnate.

To say that Wordsworth's 'Voices' sang a different tune in

ancient Greek times, however, does not mean that they were silent. The typical Greek city of the archaic period commanded its own plain or area of coastal strip, where there was enough room to grow the crops on which it depended for its subsistence. It was an oasis of human skill surrounded by the wild and unpredictable elements of mountain and sea. This consciousness may have helped shape the sharp distinction that runs through Greek religious thought between the rational and controllable world of men and the irrational but very much more powerful forces of the divine; and in their own way perhaps the Voices did speak for Liberty. Different Greek cities had different internal régimes ranging from full democracy to tight aristocracy, but thanks to their geographical circumstances they were for the most part independent and in control of their own destinies. Without this independence they could not have developed the self-confidence and political vitality for which the world has ever since remembered them.

The olive and the vine

Greece has a Mediterranean climate, and produces the normal Mediterranean crops. But the most distinctively Greek of them is, and was, the olive. It was cultivated in Greece from very early times. Equipment for the production of olive oil has recently been found in the small town or village of Myrtos in south Crete, which was occupied from about 2500 to 2170 BC. From the number of large storage vessels found, the excavator estimates that there must have been at least 1,000 trees under cultivation. During the next millennium, throughout the great period of Minoan and Mycenaean civilisation, plentiful evidence attests an extensive production of olive oil, which may even have been exported to Egypt and elsewhere in the Near East. Cultivation of the olive survived the Dark Age that followed the collapse of the Mycenaean palaces, and has flourished ever since. It spread from Greece to Italy and Egypt in the last few centuries BC, and then to other Mediterranean countries; but the olive still holds its place in Greece with 79 million trees.

The olive is an important food. According to a survey taken in 1949 it was then supplying 29 per cent of the total calory intake of the population of Crete (while cereals supplied only $33\frac{1}{3}$ per cent). In antiquity olive oil had several other uses – as an embrocation, as a vehicle for perfume, and above all as a fuel for lamps. If we add together the parts played in modern life by butter, cooking fat, soap, and paraffin, we shall appreciate what the olive meant to the ancient Greeks.

An almost equally distinctive Greek crop was the grape. Unlike the domesticated olive, which may have been developed in Greece, the domesticated vine and the art of winemaking were probably imported. However, the import must have been a very early one, for wine seems to have been produced in Greece during the Early Bronze Age. It certainly was during the Middle and Late Bronze Age, when it was of much the same order of importance in the Minoan and Mycenaean palaces as the olive. In classical antiquity Greece was famous for its wines, and remained so through medieval times. It is still a large-scale producer, though the wide diffusion that the vine has enjoyed in the Roman and modern world means that Greek wines are relatively less well known than they were.

Olives and vines may have been the main cause of the tremendous prosperity of the Aegean in the Bronze Age. Their exploitation needed a higher level of expertise, but was at the same time far more labour-saving than the cultivation of the cereals and pulses introduced by the neolithic agricultural revolution. But their economic importance, however great, is not all. They can be looked at less bleakly. 'Wine and olive oil', said the elder Pliny in the first century AD, 'are the two liquids that the human body finds most congenial, the one for internal and the other for external use.' It was in this spirit that the Greeks were grateful for them, attributing their presence in Greece to divine intervention. The vine, they alleged, was brought by Dionysus, the olive created by Athena, the one the son and the other the daughter of the King of the Gods, Zeus.

4

How They Organised Themselves

The political unit

THE nation is our normal political unit, but in ancient Greece it was the city. There are several differences between the two. The first is size. The largest city-state was much smaller than all but the tiniest of modern nations. Another difference concerned the border. Whereas most modern nations speak a different language from their neighbours, all Greek cities spoke Greek, even if the dialects varied. The main difference, however, was one of pattern. Modern countries contain a number of large towns and cities, but the Greek city (*pólis*, the source of our word politics), though it might possess a considerable tract of surrounding countryside, stood alone. If its population grew, it might found a new and independent city somewhere else, but it did not create a new city in its own territory. Cities in the classical period varied in total population from a few thousand to a hundred thousand, and the two largest of them, Athens and Syracuse, seem to have reached a quarter of a million or more. The area of Attica, the territory of Athens, was some 900 square miles, that of a normal large city would have been less than half this, and a small city might not have possessed more than 3–4 square miles altogether.

The city-state was at the height of its development in the archaic and early classical periods. Then power passed to larger entities. The transition was gradual, to begin with nothing more than treaties between cities of an increasingly per-

46

manent nature. The most famous but by no means the first of
these experiments in collaboration was the Delian League, first
formed as a security pact after the Persian Wars in 478 BC to
keep in being the military alliance against Persia, but gradually
becoming an empire under the control of its richest and most
powerful member, Athens. The other cities that belonged to the
League continued to enjoy freedom in the management of their
own affairs, but if they failed in their obligations to the League,
they could be punished with brusqueness and brutality. The
empire was dismembered in 404 BC when Athens lost the
Peloponnesian War, yet within a few years it had begun to
re-form, and its power and prosperity in the fourth century
became almost as great as they had been in the fifth.

Many other federations, some loosely knit and some with
rigid constitutions, were created in the fifth and fourth centuries. Some even had purpose-built capital cities, Brasilias of
antiquity, like the Arcadian Megalopolis (whose name, meaning 'great city', was ridiculed in a contemporary joke that
compared the city to a 'great desert'). In these federations the
normal practice was for foreign relations to be the concern of
the federal government while the cities kept their independence
as far as possible in local affairs.

However, what finally dethroned the city-state as a wielder
of independent power was not the growth of federalism but
military conquest. Macedon, a semi-barbarous northern kingdom with a Greek ruling house, had from the end of the fifth
century become both culturally and economically more and
more a part of the Greek world. Eventually it was to become a
threat to it. Philip II, an ambitious and indefatigable king, by
dint of dynastic marriages, diplomatic alliances, and military
victories, made himself, by 346 BC, a first-class power. A pact
was concluded between him and Athens, but it did not last.
Philip gained a decisive victory at Chaeronia in 338 BC, and the
rest of Greece fell to him in consequence. Henceforth the great
powers in the Greek world were the kingdom of Macedon and
(after the tremendous conquests in the East made by Philip's
son, Alexander the Great) the so-called 'successor' or 'Helleni-

stic' kingdoms in Egypt, Syria, and Asia Minor. Eventually these in their turn passed under the still wider empire of Rome, and the world of city-states had become the world of the Eternal City.

In retrospect the ever-increasing size of the ancient world's political unit is clear enough. It was not so obvious at the time. Under the Macedonian kings, and even under the Roman Empire, the Greek cities were allowed to retain their local freedoms and their own constitutions. Officially they were not subjects of the super-power but allies living under its protection. Language had an influence in the matter too, for Greek political vocabulary had been developed in the days of the city-state, and it never accommodated itself to the larger units of the later world. One could, as it were, say 'friends' and 'Romans', but one could never say 'countrymen', not even to the end of antiquity, only 'citizens'. Above all the city-state kept its place in the heart. The ancient Greek never thought of himself as belonging to his village, or to his geographical area, or to his king if he had one. He belonged to his city.

Impressions of Minoan seal-stones, reproduced approximately twice their actual size: (A) A ship, from a steatite prism seal of the early palaces (c eighteenth century BC); (B) Chalcedony seal of the period of the late palaces (c sixteenth century BC); (C) A seal of the same period showing a fish.

Minoan wine-making equipment from a Minoan country house at Zathypetro, south of Arkhanais in central Crete (c1500 BC).

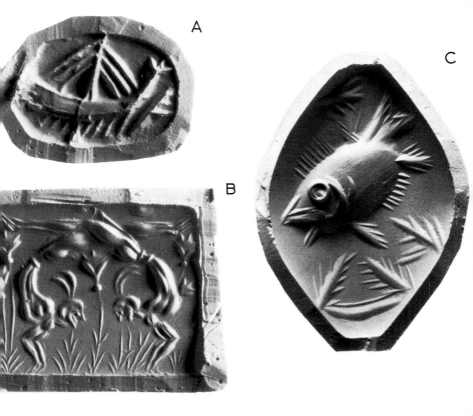

Types of government

The typical Greek city, according to the typical Greek view of the classical period, evolved through four stages – monarchy; oligarchy ('the rule of the few'); tyranny (dictatorship, generally a populist one); and, as a culminating glory or a final decadence, depending on your point of view, democracy ('the power of the people'). Ideologically in the fifth century the main division was between oligarchy and democracy, and the Peloponnesian War between Athens and Sparta and their allies was seen as a conflict between the two.

The truth was naturally less tidy than this image. There were several hundred independent cities, and each had its own history. There was constant political experiment – evolutionary, revolutionary, practical (every new colony had to be equipped with a new constitution), and visionary (ideal states, past, present, and future, were a favourite topic for publicists and writers). The results were both exciting and bewildering – exciting for the high level of constitutional refinement, bewildering for the number and variety of constitutions.

Nevertheless there were polarities, and the opposition between oligarch and democrat was real enough. Oligarchic attitudes were much the same as what we now call right-wing attitudes. The democratic side, however, cannot be called left-

---

Geometric amphora from Athens (c800 BC).

Proto-Attic amphora (700–680 BC).

D

wing. Its primary aim was not to abolish or even to equalise private property but to neutralise its political effects, and to see that rich and poor not only had the same rights in theory but also participated equally in the practice of government.

DEMOCRACY

The characteristics of Greek democracy

Aristotle, whose school collected and published the constitutions of 158 Greek cities, described the main characteristics by which a state could be classified as a democracy, as follows:

1 Every citizen is eligible for office.
2 Every citizen actually holds office in an equitably arranged system of rotation.
3 For offices filled by election the electorate is the whole citizen body, not a section of it.
4 The only such offices are those needing specialised knowledge or experience, like military commands.
5 All other offices are filled by random selection, ie by lot.
6 Offices are held on a brief tenure.
7 Sovereignty rests with the assembly of citizens, not with the holder or holders of any office.
8 Courts (Greek practice did not distinguish between judge and jury) are selected from the whole citizen body, especially for important cases.
9 Attendance in the Assembly and law courts, and services in office are all paid for.

This list shows how thoroughgoing the concept of democracy was. No modern government, and scarcely any modern corporate body, club, or association, comes anywhere near to being democratic in the Greek sense.

The only one of Aristotle's 158 case studies that we possess, and that only thanks to a papyrus discovered in 1890, is his description of the Athenian constitution. But this is not too much of a handicap. Our knowledge of other democracies, though fragmentary, is enough to show that the Athenian version was broadly typical. In looking at it one feels the same wonder that an ancient Greek might have felt if shown a modern motor car, with its neatness of design, its accurately engineered parts, and its ingenious provision for a host of eventualities.

Athenian democracy: (a) the classification of citizens

An Athenian citizen of classical times belonged by birth to one of ten tribes. Despite their name these were arbitrary divisions named after ancient heroes, much like the sections among which new boys at a school or a training camp may find themselves distributed. Within the tribe he also belonged to a *trittys* ('third'). A trittys was a geographical area, something like an English county or a French *département* but much smaller, and there were thirty of them, divided into three classes – ten urban, ten coastal, and ten rural. One trittys from each of these differently oriented groups made up a tribe. The system was instituted by the reforms of Cleisthenes at the end of the sixth century, and the criss-crossing of local loyalties was a deliberate device to strengthen the fabric of the state as a whole. Or so at least Aristotle assures us. A full democracy, he says,

> is helped by social engineering of the type employed by Cleisthenes when he reinforced the Athenian democracy and by the reformers who established democracy at Cyrene. New and more numerous tribes and other social groupings must be created. Private cults must be reduced in number and made less exclusive. Every ingenuity must be exercised to create the most thorough possible mixture of classes and to break down pre-existing associations.

The trittys was in its turn composed of a number of *demes* or parishes. These were the basic units of the political organisation of ancient Athens, and there were more than 150 of them. Each deme was responsible for its own local administration. Regular deme meetings were held and an official register of deme members kept. Indeed it was by virtue of belonging to a deme that one qualified as an Athenian citizen. The deme also gave the nearest equivalent an Athenian had to a surname – x, son of y, of deme z being the style by which all Athenians were officially known. Membership of demes went by heredity, not residence, and this must have gradually eroded the geographical basis of Cleisthenes' original system. Nevertheless this does not seem to have been felt as a practical inconvenience, and though the number of demes was increased as the population grew no basic alterations were made in the structure of deme, trittys, and tribe.

The young citizen was officially enrolled into his deme at the age of 18. He was then eligible for the Assembly, though he could not hold office or be a council member until he was 30. He was also liable for military service, and remained liable for it until he was 59. He then had one year as an Arbitrator, which meant that his services could be called on by the competent magistrate to mediate in private suits and if possible to settle them out of court. At 60 he was free from the obligation of further public service.

Athenian democracy: (b) public office

Military and administrative officers were appointed from the citizen body either by election or by lottery. Election, the less frequent method, was mainly confined to military commands. Ten divisional commanders, one for each tribe, were elected by the Assembly and empowered to appoint their own company captains. At a higher level of responsibility there were ten elected generals, five being assigned statutory posts, and five being left without portfolio, to be given whatever commission the current situation might demand. In all cases the tenure was for a year, subject to monthly confirmation by the Assembly. Nevertheless generalship was the most important office in Athens. In the field its holder had full disciplinary powers, which included the power to cashier and to inflict summary fines; and at home in the Assembly he had, naturally enough, an aura of personal authority from his office, especially if he had held it for a number of years (and there was no bar to re-election). A general was thus able to exert considerable political influence.

Other elective offices ranged from cavalry commands to reading aloud whatever documents needed to be read aloud to the Council and the Assembly. Election for the latter office was presumably a commonsense provision to prevent the lot landing on a man who stammered, or even, since literacy was not universal, a man who could not read. More important, in the fifth century, the office of chief clerk to the government was by election, and we may guess that he exercised much unobtrusive power behind the scenes. Later, however, this office was made subject to the lot, a change showing how satisfactory the Athenians must have found their method of random distribution of offices, astonishing though it may appear to us.

Astonishing or not, it was certainly their normal practice. In the developed form of the constitution (reached before the middle of the fifth century) only some three dozen offices were elective. The remainder, over 200 of them, were assigned by annual lottery. Boards of ten were the usual representative bodies, one member coming from each tribe. There were Boards of Treasurers (a property qualification was needed for these), Receivers of Revenue, Municipal Superintendents charged with the cleanliness and safety of the streets, Market Inspectors to supervise the purity of commodities sold, Inspectors of Weights and Measures, Police Commissioners, and Enforcement Officers to see that court orders were carried out. There were thirty (later forty) Circuit Judges to settle minor cases and refer others to an Arbitrator, and Legal Officers to arrange the daily working of the main law courts. There was a Board of Highway Maintenance, and Boards for the organisation of public ceremonies, religious festivals, games, and music competitions. Before entering office the official designate had to prove that he was a citizen in good standing. Once in office, the presence of colleagues, strangers yet fellow-citizens, would have put him on his best behaviour and kept him up to the accepted standards of honesty and efficiency. At the end he had to answer for his conduct in both respects, particularly if his office had entailed the handling of public money. Nobody was allowed to hold the same civil office twice.

Athenian democracy: (c) the governing bodies

The sovereign body of the state was the Assembly of all citizens. It met approximately every 9 days (the classical Greeks had no week, a later importation from the Semitic world). Any citizen could speak in it, but discussion was limited to an agenda that had previously been approved by the Council.

The Council was a body of 500, chosen annually by lot, comprising fifty members from each tribe and with the demes represented in proportion to their sizes so as to make the Council a 'miniature city', as an ancient commentator called it. Nevertheless its membership seems, from some Council lists that have been partially preserved, to have been weighted slightly, but significantly, in favour of the rich. This would have been impossible on the pure chance of the lot, so how did it happen? The probable answer is that it was up to the individual citizen whether or not he put his name down for the ballot, and the poor may have tended to refrain. The need to register one's name (which existed for jury service and probably also for the allotment of administrative offices) seems inconsistent with the theory of pure democracy. We do not know, however, if it was considered to have had any anti-democratic effects in practice.

The Council had its own Council House (see Fig 3), and met every working day of the year. Its various duties included the preliminary vetting of officials and the subsequent examination of their record in office; the supervision of the different Boards in the execution of their duties, in particular those concerned with public finance and military, especially naval, preparedness; the administration of poor relief, for those unable to work received 2 obols a day, subject to a means test; and approval of the Assembly agenda.

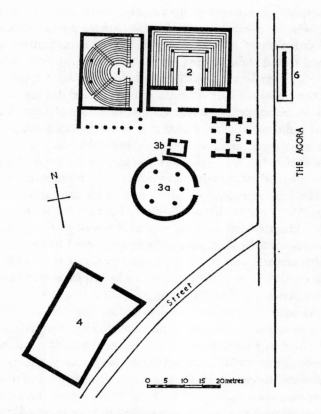

The political centre of Athens in the classical period

1   New Council House (*bouleuterion*) – built c400 BC

2   Old Council House, afterwards used as Public Records Office (*metroon*)

3 (a) Chamber of the Duty Prytany (*tholos*) – built c465 BC
  (b) Kitchen attached to *tholos*

4   The Headquarters of the Generals (*strategeion*) – built in the fifth century

5   Formal entrance to government area (*propylon*) – built c430 BC

6   Official notice boards surmounted by statues of the mythical or historical figures after whom the ten Athenian tribes were named (*Eponymous Heroes*) – latter part of fourth century

The body that drew up this agenda, and that for the Council itself, was the nearest equivalent in Athens to the cabinet or administration of a modern state. It was a committee of the Council called the Prytany, and consisted of the fifty members of one of the tribes. Each Prytany held office for a tenth of the year, the period of four Assemblies in fact, and during this time it was in permanent session. Its members dined together in a special building at public expense. It received all official state communications, heralds, and embassies. Each day it chose (by lot) a President, who was on duty for the 24 hours, together with a third of the members of the Prytany, nominated by himself. He kept the keys of the sanctuaries containing public money, the keys of the public records, and the public seal of Athens. He presided over the Council meeting of the day, and the meeting of the Assembly if there happened to be one (after the fifth century this procedure was further refined and all he had to do was to supervise the lottery by which a chairman was selected from another Prytany). The President of the Duty Prytany was thus head of the state administration for the day. It was, however, a brief moment of authority, divested both of glory, since its tenure was due to the accident of the lot, and of ambition, since the office could not be held ever again. In order to calculate the exact chance that each citizen stood of reaching the position we should need to know much more about population figures and patterns of life expectancy than we do; but if we assume that the average citizen enrolment was around 1,000 a year, then one in every two or three citizens could expect to hold the office during his lifetime.

Athenian democracy: (d) the law courts

The arrangements made for the law courts show even more clearly the elaborate and efficient fairness of Athenian democracy. One major difference from modern practice was the absence of a professional judge. Another was the size of the jury, which was never less than 200; the norm was 500, and in important cases this could be doubled or tripled. Several

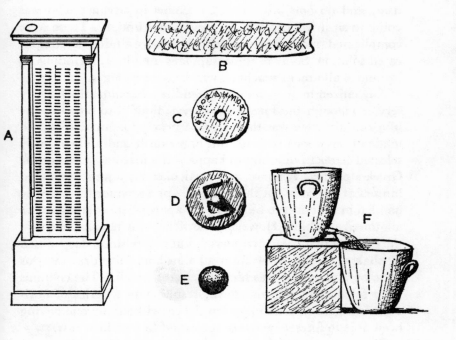

The machinery of an Athenian court

A Allotment machine (*kleroterion*)
B Juror's ticket with his name and deme
C Pierced bronze ballot, inscribed 'Voting Counter: public property' (*psephos demosia*)
D Unpierced bronze ballot, showing the other side inscribed with a letter of the alphabet
E Ball for use in the allotment machine
F Water-timer for limiting the length of speeches (*klepsydra*)

courts sat each day. The numbers involved presented a formidable problem of organisation, especially as every court had to include an equal number from each tribe (to prevent favouritism) and no one was allowed to know in advance who was going to sit in what court (to prevent corruption). These were complicated requirements, and they necessitated a complicated solution. Some of the equipment used in it, including an ingenious allotment machine, can be seen in Fig 4.

Any citizen in good standing could register annually for jury service (though the total number was limited to 6,000 in the fifth century). He was then given a ticket (tongue-shaped and made of boxwood) with his full name on it and an arbitrarily selected letter from alpha to kappa – the first ten letters of the Greek alphabet. When on any particular day a juror presented himself at the courts at the entrance appointed for his tribe, he handed in his ticket to be put in the appropriate column on the allotment machine. However, the ticket was not put there in the order of first come first served, but in a position determined by shaking and drawing from a ballot box. (The drawing was done by a man who was himself selected by lot!) The columns were filled from the top down, resulting in a series of horizontal rows each containing ten tickets without anyone having been able to foresee which ticket would be in which row.

The next stage was to choose the required number of jurymen for the business of the day. A court of 500 would need five rows from each tribe, a court of 200 two rows, and so on. White balls for the number of rows needed, and black balls for the number of rows surplus to requirement, were put through a hopper. If the first ball out was a black one, the owners of the tickets in the first row were rejected. If it was white, they were obliged to serve. Their names were called out (the process would have been quite a quick one, since it was carried out simultaneously on twenty different machines, two for each tribe), and those selected passed through into the court area, collecting a colour-coded pass to tell them which of the five or more courts they were to sit in. Once in the court, the jurors appointed four tellers (by lot) to count the votes that they would be casting at the end of the trial, five men to organise the payment of the jurymen's fee, and one man to supervise the water-clock. This was a device to give equal opportunity to each side by allowing them each the same time for presenting their arguments.

The business of the day was arranged and the allotment of the juries supervised by a board of ten officials, and from them the president of each court was chosen, also of course by lot.

The court's verdict was reached by secret ballot. In the fifth century there were two urns, one for guilty and one for not guilty, and each juror threw his voting counter (originally a pebble) into one of them. This system was later improved, when the jurors were given two bronze voting counters, one (for the plaintiff) with a hole in it and the other (for the defendant) unpierced. The urns changed their function, one being used for the votes that counted and the other for the discards. Thus each juryman had to drop a counter into each urn, and nobody could tell by listening to the tinkle which way any particular individual had voted.

As for the quality of Athenian justice, the jurymen took an oath to vote according to the law where law existed and to the best of their judgement where it did not, to judge the point at issue, and to listen without prejudice to both sides. There is no reason to suppose that they did not carry out this oath. Comedians joked, men who lost their case protested, and posterity has sometimes condemned the whole system outright because of the one trial of Socrates, but the more one reads what was written at the time (and we possess a large number of speeches made to fourth-century Athenian courts) the more one is impressed with the stability of the system, its capacity to deal with financial intricacies as well as points of principle, and above all with the general trust in which it was held.

Democratic values

Laws were publicly recorded on stone inscriptions, and anybody could go and read them to discover his legal position. This was considered a major guarantee of justice and equality.

'With written laws', says Theseus, the mythical founder of Athens, in Euripides' play *The Suppliant Women*, 'rich and poor are on an equal footing. Both can speak freely and the one who wins his case will be the one with right on his side, not money.'

Theseus, in this scene, is defending his city of Athens against the contempt of a foreigner. In addition to equality before the law the main points he makes are the equal political power given by the rotation of offices, the opportunity for glory given to every individual by the right to speak on public questions in the Assembly, and the general security of life and property that is guaranteed by a democratic government. This last point may surprise us, but it was evidently an accepted argument in favour of democracy, and we find it used by others, among them Lysias, a rich businessman who became a lawyer, and the philosopher Aristotle.

OLIGARCHY

Oligarchic values

The case against democracy put forward by the foreigner in Euripides' scene consists mainly of sneers against the horror of mob rule and the havoc that can be wreaked by an unprincipled, uneducated, and unpropertied demagogue. Euripides is not the best authority for anti-democratic arguments, since he was a democrat himself. Nevertheless this was how genuine oligarchs argued. 'In every land', says the author of a late fifth-century tract on the Athenian constitution, 'the better classes oppose democracy. This is because the better classes have the most respect for morality, law, and the higher values of life, whereas the people have no education, no self-discipline, and no principles.' The favourite constitutions of the oligarchs were those of Sparta and the cities of Crete.

Sparta and Crete

The keynote of these societies was order. Boys were boys, not precocious adults. The old were to be deferred to. Foreigners were unwelcome or excluded altogether. Subject classes, which existed in both Sparta and Crete, were kept firmly in their place. The citizens too knew where they stood, and spent most of their lives as part of a clearly defined military hierarchy.

In Sparta the military routine began early. From his seventh year till he was 30 the future citizen was totally involved in what was by all accounts a brutal training, suffering it till he was 20 and then administering it. Even after this, though he was now an adult citizen, free to marry, look after his estates, and enjoy some normal life, he had to dine communally in an army mess and to continue in training. The régime had some democratic aspects, as Aristotle points out, for rich and less rich had the same food in their messes, wore the same clothing, and had their sons educated together. There was also a democratic side to the political constitution: there was a Council chosen by the citizens, and the most important administrative officers were five annually elected ephors. But the oligarchic features predominated. Aristotle singles out the powers of inflicting death or banishment being vested in a small number of magistrates, and the fact that all offices went by election, none by lot. The oligarchic atmosphere of Sparta was intensified by the great inequality of landed wealth (none other was permitted) which grew up among the citizens and which eventually caused a drastic decline in population. Sparta also possessed royalty, and in a strange form. There was not just one royal house, but two, and consequently two kings. They not merely reigned but ruled, subject to some constitutional safeguards enforced by the ephors, who also had the duty of resolving disagreements between them.

The cities of Crete were also controlled by tightly knit oligarchies. The presence of a subject population, the relative smallness of the citizen body, its military life and communal messing, were points in common between Crete and Sparta. But whereas Sparta was always at the head of leagues and alliances and claimed to be the champion of Greece against the encrouching power of Athens, Crete in classical times was a comparatively placid backwater. Its ruling military class seems

to have been less brutalised than that of Sparta and more ready
to enjoy the pleasures of its position – at least if a song attributed
to a Cretan called Hybrias reflects a mood that was common
among its members:

> *I've lots of money, spear and sword,*
> *And a shield to save my skin.*
> *These tread my wine, and sow my corn,*
> *And bring my harvest in.*

> *But others haven't spear or sword,*
> *Or a shield to save their skin.*
> *They clasp my feet, call me their lord,*
> *Their king and sovereign.*

Ancient Greek political theories

In addition to the several hundred constitutions, oligarchic
and democratic, which existed in the cities of the Greek world,
there were others proposed by political theorists that existed
only in the mind. Some of them had practical application in
view. For instance, Phaleas of Chalcedon suggested the gradual
and painless equalisation of property by allowing the rich to
give but not to receive dowries, and the poor to receive them
but not to give them. A similarly modest proposal in the oligarchic interest, mentioned by Aristotle, is that instead of everyone having an equal vote, the vote should be weighted in
accordance with the voter's tax assessment. Others put forward
schemes for total change. The most famous of them is Plato,
who designed two versions of his ideal state, one uncompromis-
ingly utopian in the *Republic* and one less high-flying in the
Laws. Plato's ideal state was extreme both ways. It went beyond
democracy in imposing absolute communism, not only of
property, but also of women and children. It went beyond
oligarchy in imposing an absolute social hierarchy buttressed

against change by a rigid censorship of all art, music, and literature. It makes heady reading, and it has inspired many a moralist and many a philosopher, but if Plato's idealism is unmatched in its kind, so is the relentlessly sober critique of it by his pupil Aristotle. Aristotle's objections were partly practical, showing why community of children would not work and how the abolition of private property would create inefficiency and neglect, cause more corruption than it claimed to cure, and destroy much human happiness. But his most interesting argument is aimed at the basic proposition of Plato's utopia, that the greater the unity of a city the better. Aristotle makes the point that a city is not an organisation with a single purpose like a military alliance, but a balance of independent interests. As variety is its essence, the less unity it has the better.

The image of Greek democracy today

Greek political philosophy is still a live subject. Plato and Aristotle have keen followers, either at first hand or through the schools of political thought, totalitarian or pluralist, which they have helped form. The same cannot be said for the study of actual Greek political experience. This has usually been dismissed as irrelevant, except for purely academic curiosity. The reason most often heard today is that Greek society was based on slavery and that this made its democracies a sham – they involved only a minority of the total population, and were only workable anyway because the citizens did not have to spend their time earning a living. It is difficult to judge the first part of this argument, since we do not know the proportion of slave to free even in Athens, let alone in other cities. All one can say is that their democracies did not seem like a sham to the Greeks themselves. The other part is manifestly false. The majority of Athenian citizens undoubtedly did work for their living, and the provision of 500 Council members together with 250 or so officers of state cannot be considered an excessive burden for a citizen body which on any estimate must have numbered some tens of thousands.

The argument that Greek democracy is invalidated by Greek slavery is a fairly recent one. Before it became fashionable, other arguments were used to the same end. One was that assemblies of the whole citizen body are not possible in communities the size of a modern state. Television, telephones, and electronic calculators have now removed much of the force of this objection, but in any case the assembly of all citizens was only one element out of many in a democratic constitution; and since no private societies or institutions meet the ancient criteria of democracy, however small their numbers, one may suspect that this particular objection was never a genuine one. Another way of discounting Greek experience used to be to say that the Greeks were fine philosophers but incapable as practical men. This is the Roman stereotype of the Greeks, but, just or unjust, it is totally irrelevant to the Greeks in the days of their power.

Other grounds for condemning Athenian democracy have been that it dominated an empire and was therefore hypocritical, or the opposite, that it lost the Peloponnesian War and was therefore inefficient. Stranger, but seriously argued, grounds have been that it gave material for the satire of comic poets or that it displeased Plato. Perhaps the most astonishing

---

The Temple of Apollo at Corinth, sixth century BC.

The Pirene fountain at Corinth, ancient even in the eyes of the classical Greeks. Most of what can be seen today is Roman restoration or embellishment. The courtyard in the foreground with the great basin in the middle was the gift of Herodes Atticus, a millionaire of the second century AD, and the marble columns in front of the arches are a Byzantine addition.

of all is the scornful dismissal of its importance by the scholar who first edited the newly discovered papyrus of Aristotle's *Athenian Constitution* on behalf of the British Museum. 'There is not much profit', he wrote, 'to be derived from minutely studying the political proceedings of the Greek states. The Greeks had none of that genius for organisation which distinguishes the Romans . . . At Athens above all there was no aptitude for the sobriety, the conservatism, the adherence to form, which are essential for the solid building up of a political constitution.' This, when he was editing a treatise which gives on every page evidence for meticulous organisation, when Athens was notorious in the Greek world for her pride in her antiquity and her traditions, and when the most superficial glance at the calendar of history will show that the days of the power and glory of Athens lasted from Solon to Alexander the Great, a period of 250 years, longer than has been vouchsafed to most states in the world, to say nothing of the long constitutional evolution that must have taken place before the start of recorded history or of the 500 years of continued and not altogether inglorious prosperity that Athens enjoyed after she had passed from the stage as a major world power.

When the arguments in support of a conclusion keep circling,

Pirate ship on the right chasing a merchantman; an Attic black-figure cup (c530 BC).

A long-jumper and his coach; the jumper holds weights (*halteres*) in his hand and behind him is a spare pair. A rough but vigorous drawing from the inside of an Attic red-figure cup (510–500 BC).

E

and the conclusion itself remains as fixed as the northern star, we may suspect that there is prejudice at work. An ancient Greek would have had no difficulty in diagnosing its nature. He would have called it oligarchic, just as he would have called every constitutional government in the modern world oligarchic in his sense of the term. It might strike him as sad, but it would certainly not strike him as surprising, that in these circumstances the friends of Greek democracy should be so few and far between.

5

Who Did the Work

The image of the working farmer

TRADITIONALLY the core of a free city was its free citizen farmers working their own land with their own hands. In many parts of Greece this remained the pattern throughout antiquity, and elsewhere it remained powerful as an idea. In old-established cities, whenever the gap between rich and poor became too glaring, the call of the champions of the oppressed was always for a redistribution of land, and in new settlements colonists were given equal allotments (irrespective of the number of their children) on which they were expected to fend for themselves. Plenty of small farmers survived in the remote upland districts of Attica in classical times. They were stereotyped by townsmen either as country bumpkins or as sturdy peasants. A dubious character in a comedy by Aristophanes is asked if he is a farmer and replies, 'Do I look an idiot?', whereas in Euripides a working farmer is described as no beau and no townee but a true man of the type who keeps the country going.

Whatever the truth of this remark as a moral judgement, it was certainly not true economically for the more advanced parts of Greece. There were sizeable urban populations from at least the sixth century BC, and there were also large estates where the owner did not do the work himself but supervised the labour of others, or even employed farm managers to do so. Many cities as they grew found they had to import food, thus creating a class of merchants and merchant-bankers to finance

71

them. With their increasing prosperity they sucked in more and more people, both Greeks and barbarians – the former as free residents, the latter as slaves – and in cities of this kind, though doubtless the majority of citizens continued to possess some land which they looked after themselves, the image of the working farmer as the backbone of the state slipped more and more into the realm of nostalgia.

The landless man

Citizenship was no guarantee against poverty, and for all sorts of reasons a citizen might find himself without land, or without enough land for support. The most obvious way for such a citizen to make his living was by working for another – often a large landlord. The picture is drawn for us in Homer's *Iliad,* our earliest work of Greek literature. Hired harvesters mow the corn while the owner looks on in silent pleasure, and a feast is prepared for all at the end of the day. This is a happy enough scene, and there is no reason to suppose that it never took place, but harvesting is a seasonal occupation, and when the labourer was paid off, he was in a worse position than a slave unless he had a home of his own to go to or could find another job. We do not hear of employment exchanges to help him do so, but there was a regular place in Athens, called Market Mound, where casual labour went to be hired, and doubtless there were similar arrangements in other cities. Shipping could be a large employer of poorer citizens. Aristotle mentions in this connection Athens for its navy, Aegina and Chios for their merchant marines, Tenedos for passenger boats, and Tarentum and Byzantium for fishing fleets

The next step up on the economic ladder was occupied by the craftsman. His was a relatively safe life, safer than that of the rich. As a character of Menander's says:

> *A stroke of bad luck strips you of your money.*
> *What are you left with? Just a naked body!*
> *There's only one security in life,*
> *And that's to have a trade.*

There were many specialised trades – carpenters, shipwrights, plasterers, masons, stonecutters, sculptors, painters, potters, cobblers, textile-workers, fullers, tanners, dyers, smelters, smiths, and jewellers. Others, like small shopkeepers and auctioneers, though not skilled in the same sense, enjoyed much the same status and conditions of life.

A characteristic of these trades was their family nature. Ancient writers tell us this and many inscriptions confirm it. Fathers taught their sons, who would then support them in their old age. But this was not all. Such a life could give job satisfaction as well as income and security. We have many epitaphs where craftsmen boast of their skill.

Trade could lead to contact with the great, and shops in central Athens were something of a social venue. We hear of Socrates and his friends frequenting Simon the shoemaker's, and American archaeologists have discovered his very shop in the central district of Athens. Hobnails and bone eyelets for bootlaces identified the shop as a cobbler's, and it contained the broken base of a wine cup with Simon's name on it. Other craftsmen might rise to fame in their own right. Sculptors, painters, and architects (risen carpenters or masons) could gain international commissions for a temple or other sanctuary building, and their fees, at least in the fourth century (we do not know about earlier practice), could be high.

This path to wealth, assuming that it led there, was naturally restricted to very few. Another path was expansion. A craftsman who did not have a son of his own might (if he could afford it, and we know that not all could) take on a slave as a workshop apprentice to secure his business for his old age, or he might take on slaves to increase his output. In this way it was possible for small factories to develop. We hear of establishments employing twenty men (making couches), thirty (making knives and daggers), and even a hundred or more (making shields). Their owners were rich men.

Aristocrats may have disdained money made in trade, and comic poets, even in democratic Athens, made jokes about it, but it was no absolute bar to social acceptance. Socrates' father is said to have been a stonemason, Sophocles' either a smith or a carpenter. Many leading politicians came from a background of trade. Cleon and Anytus were connected with tanning, Cleophon with lyre-making, and Hyperbolus with flasks. Unfortunately we do not know the precise nature of the connections or how close the politicians themselves were to a knowledge of the crafts that had built up their family fortunes.

The rich

The highest fortunes we know of in classical Athens were between 70 and 100 talents (see pp 9–10 for a discussion of ancient money). Such a capital would have yielded an annual amount of 250–300 times a subsistence income – a large differential, though less than that enjoyed by today's ultrarich. Such wealth was rare, however, and being rich, for taxation purposes, meant having 4 talents or more. We do not know how many in Athens qualified – perhaps 2,000 persons, or approximately 1 per cent of the total population.

One possible source of wealth was manufacturing, as we have seen. Others included rent from property, the buying and selling of real estate, commerce, or banking. Socially speaking, though, the best source was land, especially if it had been held a long time, and quite a number of Athenian families enjoyed both acreage and ancestry.

Privilege has obligations. In a splendid passage in Homer the hero Sarpedon asks why he and his fellow nobles have the best food, the best wine, and the best estates. He answers himself that it is because they are prepared to risk their lives by fighting in the front line. The same spirit is made unheroically precise in Solon's constitutional provisions in sixth-century Athens. The 200 bushels-of-corn-a-year man has to provide his own armour and fight as a hoplite in the heavy infantry, but 300 bushels raises you to the cavalry and saddles you with the need to keep a horse. The burdens of office were also apportioned to income, the highest being reserved for the 500-bushel class. From the little we know of other city constitutions in archaic Greece we may guess that the same general principles applied; and though later, in Athens, democratic sentiment removed nearly all the privileged access to office of Solon's constitution, the richer man's obligation to hoplite service remained, and there also remained for the very rich an élite cavalry corps of 1,000 horse.

Normal state revenues came from customs duties, direct taxes on non-citizens, and the rent of state property (especially in the case of fifth-century Athens the silver mines at Laurium). Routine taxation was therefore not weighted against the rich, but unforeseen gaps between revenue and expenditure might arise in a crisis, and in Athens these were made good by capital levies on the rich according to a system of rotation. The rate could be fierce, rising to 20 per cent on large fortunes.

A more exciting tax on the rich (those with over 4 talents) was the liturgy. This required personal service as well as financial outlay. One form of it was a year's command of a naval trireme. The ship itself and the crew's wages were provided from public funds, but not the care and maintenance. The cost would generally work out at just under a talent. Another liturgy was to head the official delegation to a religious festival, such as the Olympic Games, and a third was financing a tragedy, a comedy, or a dithyrambic chorus (where choirs, men or boys, sang specially composed odes in competition). These liturgies could cost between $\frac{1}{4}$ and $\frac{3}{4}$ talent. There were grumbles, of course, and the man who told an Athenian court, 'I have no complaint. If we are rich we ought to serve the public', sounds more sanctimonious than convincing. There is a more authentic ring about another remark, made when the unpleasant son of a naturalised banker had run into unexpected expense during his command of a trireme. 'At last!' exclaimed one of his colleagues. 'The rat is tasting the trap – he always wanted to be an Athenian citizen!' Nevertheless by performing one's liturgy well there was glory to be had, both for oneself and for one's city. And doubtless enjoyment too, which is more than can be said for most taxpaying.

Women of citizen class

The same rich banker's unpleasant son – his name was
Apollodorus and he was forever engaged in litigation – told a
court, 'We have mistresses for pleasure, prostitutes for relief,
and wives to give us children and to look after our houses.'
This, though coarsely put, was true enough. The proper place
for an Athenian's daughter who became an Athenian's wife
was undoubtedly the home. Outside it she had no powers. She
was always the ward of a male guardian, could not attend the
Assembly, serve in the law courts, or make a binding contract
for more than routine amounts. Finally, if her husband died,
she might find herself bequeathed to another.

The economic contribution made by a woman of citizen class
was therefore normally confined to the services she rendered
within her own household. These included milling flour, bak-
ing, and other food preparation, spinning, weaving, and the
making of clothes – not a negligible contribution. Moreover in
case of need she could exploit her domestic skills to earn a cash
income, and we know that this was done. The wives of poorer
citizens often had a stall in the market where they sold what
they made at home. A wife who was married to a shopkeeper
could help in the shop, and a wife could even help on occasions
on the farm.

In compensation for the restricted life she was forced to lead,
an Athenian woman had considerable security, thanks to the
dowry system. The dowry, which might be anything from a few
hundred drachmae to a talent or more in the case of a rich
man's daughter, was returnable if the husband treated her
badly and the marriage broke down. Thus the wife had a lever
of power, and it is clear enough from the literature of the time
that there was nothing strange to the Athenian in the idea of
wives being strong-willed and formidable. It is clear too from
speeches in the Athenian law courts that wives often knew all
about their family finances and might even represent their
husband's family at family financial conferences. Epitaphs tell
us that there was plenty of natural affection between husbands
and wives, and we have Demosthenes' word for it that quar-

relling partners were often reconciled for the children's sake. So Athenian marriages could be quite like our own, despite the different legal framework, and an Athenian woman's life could be a satisfying one. But there were two important conditions: first that a suitable dowry could be found for her, and second that she was prepared to fit into her conventional place in society.

THE CITIZEN ABROAD

Free movement

'Much travelled . . . he saw many cities, and knew the ways of many men.' So Homer introduced his hero in the *Odyssey*. Other heroes of myth and legend had knocked about the world too – Jason in his ship *Argo*, Theseus, Heracles, even Paris, the seducer of Helen. The idea of free movement was thus familiar enough to the Greeks.

So was its practice. Religious festivals were great occasions of personal travel. There was also travel on business or trade, both within Greece and beyond, colonisation, and the reverse process by which growing cities attracted skilled immigrants. All these factors made for the movement of people, and the normal reactions developed for dealing with it. Hospitality was a virtue ('Welcome the coming, speed the parting guest' is a maxim from Homer, made English by Alexander Pope), but there was also suspicion. As Euripides makes Medea say, a stranger must be cautious and conform. There was the same ambivalence in corporate attitudes. Cities accorded special privileges to foreigners, but they could also close ranks against them, even to the extent of expelling them altogether, as happened in Sparta.

The migrant worker

The migrant worker, resident for a short time only, was one class of non-citizen in a Greek community. His work might be with the brain or with the hand. Poets, reciters of poetry, philosophers, educationists, and public lecturers of all sorts travelled either at the invitation of kings or nobles or else on their own account to public festivals in order to compete for a prize. Doctors travelled for the sake of experience and employment. Manual trades like stonecutting could also take their practitioners abroad. The craftsmen who built the great temples erected by prosperous communities from Sicily to Asia Minor were by no means all local, even in the larger cities, and certainly not when the site was in the open countryside or comparatively remote. If craftsmen had to be enticed from abroad on such occasions, how much more necessary was it to bring in sculptors, painters, and architects. The tradition continued into the Roman Empire, and we have many epitaphs of itinerant craftsmen who tell us how many cities they had worked in.

The metics

It was possible to settle in a city not one's own, and in some cities such as Athens there was a special legal status for persons of transferred domicile ('metics' from the Greek *metoikoi*). Obligations like tax-paying and military service were balanced against privileges like the right to use the courts. In Athens marrying a citizen and owning land were not usually allowed, though permission might be granted as an extra privilege.

The metics of Athens counted among their number some of the richest inhabitants of the city. They were prominent in shipping circles and in banking. But there were lots of other occupations for a metic, from being a kept mistress (or for that matter a freelance one) to a philosopher. Aristotle, the founder of the Peripatetic School, came from Stagirus in Macedonia; Zeno, the founder of the Stoics, from Citium in Cyprus; Aristotle's successor, Theophrastus, from Lesbos; and so on. The traffic could be both ways. Epicurus' father, who came from an old Athenian family, emigrated to Samos where he became a schoolmaster, and then to Colophon in Asia Minor. Epicurus himself taught at Mytilene, and then at Lampsacus on the Dardanelles, before finally moving back to Athens and founding his own philosophic school. The sons of the Athenian potter called Bacchius, whose signature on pots is known and whose epitaph has been found, emigrated to Ephesus about 330 BC when the pottery trade in Athens was declining, and were there welcomed with a grant of full citizenship.

SLAVES

Theories of slavery

To the classical Greeks the abolition of slavery would have been as much beyond the realm of practical politics as its introduction would be for us, though there were different views about it as an institution. According to one fifth-century school of thought there had originally been no slaves at all. According to another the right state of affairs would be for every citizen to own a slave of his own. It was a matter of easy observation that some slaves were more intelligent and more trustworthy than some citizens, and this prompted doubts about the institution. Perhaps nature's slave and nature's free man, though distinct enough in theory, were sometimes wrongly classified in the real world. Aristotle adopted this position and compared master and slave to soul and body or mind and matter. Taken further, though, it could result in apathy on the ground that the legal position was essentially irrelevant; for the so-called free man might be a slave to anger or avarice, the so-called slave as wise and virtuous and free and happy in his own self as a king. This was the attitude of later philosophic sects like the Stoics and of later religions like Christianity. Roman jurists, on the other hand, took a more straightforward view of the institution, describing slavery as it was, but defining it as contrary to nature.

Historical development

Just as theories about slavery changed during antiquity, so

did its practice. Parts of classical Greece had subject populations tied to the land in a kind of serfdom, perhaps the result of
newcomers conquering earlier inhabitants or through one
section of the population gradually sinking out of sight in the
social scale. Whichever it was, serfdom is not the same as
slavery, and the one did not turn into the other. On the contrary, the subject populations existed in the more backward
and conservative areas, while slavery grew up in the progressive
democracies.

The Greeks who thought slavery a recent innovation were
perhaps right. At any rate it seems to have been much less
important in early Greece. Before the fifth century we hear only
of domestic slaves, servants and retainers within a household,
labour for harvesting and such occupations, where it is mentioned, seeming always to be hired. This does not mean that
there was no productive employment of slaves. Penelope in the
Odyssey is said to have had a family slave to look after her
orchard, as did her father-in-law Laertes. Odysseus' swineherd
Eumaeus was a captive slave, having been a nobleman (or so
he said) in the land of his birth. The distinction was not therefore between service and production, but between casual and
permanent labour. Hired free men did the former, kept slaves
the latter.

The industrial slavery of classical times that grew up in
Athens and other large cities developed from this domestic
slavery. Establishments were normally small, a few assistants
living and working with the master craftsman. Slaves of this
kind would usually be skilled workmen themselves, have wives
of their own, and enjoy freedom of movement so long as they
did not desert their master. We read in Athenian court cases of
slaves being as a matter of course in positions of considerable
trust – as clerks and secretaries handling money, as ships'
captains, even as agents in the Bosporus for shippers operating
in Athens. One extreme case was that of Phormio. He was an
untrained barbarian up for sale as a slave, and might, as the
speaker in the case says, have become a cook or some such thing.
Instead he happened to be bought by the banker Pasion, who

taught him to read and write. In due course Phormio became Pasion's chief clerk, and, when Pasion died in 370 BC, Phormio succeeded not only to the running of his master's business but also to his master's wife, from whom he had children of his own. He also became a citizen. So, as our informant puts it in a speech full of anti-slave prejudice, he ended up by being rich, well known and Greek instead of being poor, obscure and barbarian!

Slaves were also employed by the Athenian state, including, surprisingly, a corps of 300 Scythians who served as the city's police. Others were employed for the construction, repair, and maintenance of public buildings. There was not necessarily discrimination between slave and free in terms of employment. Some of the building accounts for a fifth-century temple on the Acropolis (the Erechtheum) have been discovered, and they show that the fluting of the columns of the east front was done by gangs of workmen that included citizens, metics, and slaves, and there is no apparent difference either in the work that individuals were expected to do or in the pay that they received.

Undoubtedly, though, some slaves were less comfortable than others. The least comfortable, in Athens at least, were probably those who worked in the silver mines at Laurium. These were owned by the state, but concessions to work them were leased to citizens, who might work their concessions themselves or employ their own or hired slaves. Xenophon tells us that the politician Nicias possessed 1,000 mine slaves whom he hired out for an obol a day each. This scale of operation is quite out of keeping with the rest of our evidence for fifth-century slave ownership. It is told as an exceptional case, on hearsay evidence, and 60 years after Nicias' death, but true or not it must have seemed plausible when Xenophon wrote it, about 355 BC, and the idea of numbers like this brings us within sight of the terrible and impersonal gang slavery of the great estates of the Roman world.

The importance of ancient slavery

It is a much debated question how far ancient society was based on slavery. It would be easier to answer if we had some idea of the figures involved. The only city for which we have any accurate knowledge of the number of citizens is Athens, and even for Athens modern estimates of the slave population vary widely (Table 3).

TABLE 3   ESTIMATES OF THE POPULATION (INCLUDING WOMEN AND CHILDREN) OF ATHENS AND ATTICA IN THE CLASSICAL PERIOD

	Slaves	*Metics*	*Citizens*	*Total population*
Low estimates	25,000	25,000	100,000	150,000
High estimates	100,000	40,000	160,000	300,000

We can infer from speeches from the law courts and from contemporary comedy that a poor family might have one servant or none at all, and the better off two or three but rarely more. We cannot begin to say, however, what proportion of slaves there were in domestic service, what in industry, farming, and mining. Nor can we say how much of the productive work was done by slaves and how much by free men. Ancient writers do not tell us, and they might indeed have been surprised at our wanting to know. Slavery was barely thought of as an economic factor, for what distinguished a slave from a free man was not the type of work he did or the money he got for it, but simply that he belonged to somebody else and had to do what he was told.

Economics may not have been much affected by slavery, but politics may have. Citizens in a democracy needed leisure to carry out their public duties, a problem discussed by the Greeks themselves, and the democratic answer was to pay for the time lost. For an oligarch, however, this was not enough: if a man had to work for his living he could not have time to understand political questions and should not be given political responsibility. So either every citizen should be a slave-owner or government should be reserved for the rich. Clearly the debate is an ideological one, and only touches on the necessity of slaves if we assume that slave labour was needed to finance democratic payment for office. A look at the figures suggests not. The number of office-holders, members of the Council, and an average day's court attendance could not have totalled more than 1,500, or 1 per cent of the total population, by no means an extravagant proportion to be employed in the public administration.

However, it remains a paradox that personal slavery (as opposed to serfdom) should have grown up, perhaps indeed have been invented, in those very same progressive democracies of archaic and classical Greece where the concept of personal freedom was first evolved and defined. It seems that there must be a connection. A possible explanation is that both were a product of coined money. Coins, anonymous, undiscriminating, and readily transferable, encourage independence, but they could also have encouraged slavery by making it an easy matter to buy and sell slaves at a price like any other commodity.

A more cold-blooded explanation is that slavery was part of the mechanism by which non-Greeks participated in the economically and technologically more advanced Greek world, for though Greek cities did fight each other and enslave the prisoners they took, the slavery of Greek to Greek was considered somewhat unethical and remained comparatively rare. Nearly all slaves came from abroad – Asia Minor, Thrace, the Black Sea coast, and elsewhere. Whether they were war captives, taken in deliberately mounted expeditions or supplied by a locally organised slave trade (and both means were employed), the effect was to bring barbarians into the orbit of Greek civilisation. On arrival they were normally taken into a household or taught a trade or both. Many, perhaps most, would adjust to their new surroundings well enough eventually to find themselves with a family of their own and perhaps to be granted their freedom. In a generation or so their barbarian origin would begin to be forgotten. Meanwhile by their presence and the work they performed they strengthened their host city and contributed each his mite towards making possible the tremendous expansion of Greek civilisation throughout the Mediterranean and the Near East.

As an economic phenomenon, therefore, the recent large-scale immigration into industrial Europe of workers from the undeveloped countries may provide a better analogy for classical Greek slavery than the more usually quoted importation of Africans into the American South.

School lessons shown on an Attic red-figure cup signed by the painter Duris (c485 BC). The upper illustration shows instruction in the lyre and in reading. On the left both master and pupil are seated, each holding a lyre; on the wall behind hang a cup, a spare lyre with plectrum on a lanyard tied to it, and a brazier. In the reading lesson on the right, the master holds a papyrus roll with the first line of a hexameter poem written on it, while the boy stands in front of him and the escort looks on. On the wall hangs a flute-case made of hide, another lyre and another cup.

The lower picture shows instruction in the double-flute and in writing. On the left, the master demonstrates sitting down while the boy stands. On the wall hang a papyrus roll, a set of writing tablets and a lyre. In the writing lesson on the right, the master sits with stylus and writing tablet while the boy stands and the escort looks on. On the wall is a setsquare for ruling guidelines on the tablet.

6

How They Lived

FAMILY LIFE

The unit

THE family, not the individual, was the basic unit of Greek social life, and the family was understood in a wide sense. In addition to a man's wife and children it included any household slaves (who, in Athens at least, were introduced into a house in the same way as a new bride, by being scattered with nuts and dried fruit, and thereafter allowed to share in the family religious observances). It also included a man's parents, though they might not live in the same house. A father normally resigned his headship of the family when his son married, and the son

Hermione, the literature mistress (*Hermione grammatike*). A mummy portrait from Greco-Roman Egypt, first or second century AD.

became responsible for looking after his parents. Collaterally the responsibility of the head of a family extended as far as second cousins. Nor did the concept of the family end with the living. The ancestors, and their graves, were entitled to veneration, and their cult was a major part of family life. Despite some opposition to the family by philosophers (notably the Cynics and Plato in the *Republic*), the universal testimony of everyday Greece, in speeches in the courts, in literature, and in epitaphs, shows that the family was the institution above all to which the normal Greek felt a sense of belonging, and that it was in the family if anywhere that he participated in immortality.

Only the full citizen in his own city could enjoy a full family life. Nevertheless the migrant could hope to return home, and the metic to become assimilated in his city of domicile; even the slave could look forward either to becoming an indispensable part of his master's family or to receiving his freedom and establishing a non-citizen family of his own. For all these classes the citizen's family life was the pattern of normality, setting the standard to which they aspired. Most of our evidence about it comes from Athens, and customs undoubtedly differed in detail from city to city, but it is likely that the broad lines of family life were much the same throughout Greece. Only in Sparta and Crete, with their aristocratic societies and their subject populations, do there seem to have been major differences.

The stages of life

Birth took place in the home, normally with the assistance of a midwife. We have no figures for deaths at childbirth, but we can assume from remarks in Aristotle and elsewhere that it was a dangerous time for both mother and child. Even if the child survived the experience, he was still not safe. In Sparta the newborn child of a citizen was officially inspected, and, if found defective, was not reared. Elsewhere too deformed children could be allowed to die, and so could children who were just unwanted. This was a familiar theme in myth – wit-

ness the stories of Oedipus and Paris – and a favourite device
in the plots of later comedy. In real life, though, the exposure
of healthy children was probably rare, and may even have been
virtually non-existent in the classical period. Speeches in the
Athenian courts do not mention it as a practice, though we hear
in them of plenty of men with families larger than they needed
or could properly afford.

The naming of a child took place on the tenth day after
birth, with drinking and dancing, in the presence of the rela-
tives of both sexes. There ensued the normal process of growing
up and being educated, until, at the age of 18, a boy was
officially enrolled into his deme.

The right age for marriage was a subject of debate. One of
Euripides' characters boldly says that young marriages are
much better for everyone concerned, including the future
children. Aristotle more soberly recommended 37 as the opti-
mum age for men, 18 for women – marriage ages not uncom-
mon in rural areas of Greece today. Aristotle's reasons were
partly genetic, that younger girls produce smaller and weaker
children at greater risk to themselves; partly marital, that in
this way both partners will reach the end of their child-
producing lives together; and partly social, that fathers of too
advanced an age can neither help nor be helped by their
children, while with younger fathers there will be less respect
from the son and greater likelihood of quarrelling over family
business and family finance. In practice men probably tended
to marry about the age of 30 and women about 16, with the
poor marrying their daughters somewhat earlier, the rich later.

The two things needed for a valid marriage were first that a
formal betrothal should take place in front of witnesses and then
that the couple should live together. There was regularly a
dowry, though it was given by custom not by law. This was a
capital sum from the bride's family to guarantee her maintenance, and was administered by the husband as long as the
marriage lasted. If the marriage broke down or the husband
died, then the sum reverted to the woman, to be administered
for her by the head of her own family, who then became her

guardian. If she remarried, it was then available again as her new dowry. Only if she died first, did the dowry remain with her husband.

Marriages were arranged, and in theory a woman had no say in the choice of her husband. A widow could even be left to another in her husband's will. In practice, though, particularly among the upper classes, a woman with a mind of her own seems to have had some opportunity to exercise it. Where the family was without a male heir, however, matters were different. Then the daughter, who was the heiress, was expected to marry her nearest male relative, generally her father's brother, in order to preserve the continuity of the household, and such marriages were put through officially by the judgement of a public court.

On the death of the head of a household the family property passed to the son. If there was more than one son, it was shared between them, and in this way new families could come into being. If there were only daughters, the preservation of the family was guaranteed by the arrangement just outlined. Only if the head of a family was childless was there a danger of his household being extinguished, but in this case he could adopt an heir, either during his lifetime or by will. The adoption of such an heir, often a relative, was essentially a device to preserve the house. The heir was expected to marry and beget a son, and when he had done so, he could, if he wished, move back into his own family. In the meantime, though, he had to renounce any family expectations of his own, so that the possibility of two houses being merged could never arise. In compensation for this, if he was adopted in the lifetime of the head of a house to whom sons were subsequently born, he inherited an equal share with the natural heirs.

The effect of these various Athenian laws and customs relating to marriage and inheritance was to keep up the number of separate families. The state's primary interest in the matter was to preserve the number of those liable for military, civic, and religious duties, but keeping families from merging or dying out will have also helped to preserve a more even distribution of wealth. In Sparta, where the same provisions did not apply and women were able to inherit property in their own right, there was an increasing tendency for wealth to be concentrated in fewer and fewer hands as rich men without sons married their daughters to rich sons-in-law. This meant fewer landowners, and fewer landowners (because Spartan citizens had to have property) meant fewer citizens. According to Aristotle, and there is no reason to doubt him, the custom of female inheritance was in this way the prime cause of the decline in the number of citizens, which by the middle of the fourth century seems to have been only 20 per cent of what it had been at the beginning of the fifth, and this decline led to the ultimate collapse of Sparta as a significant power in the Greek world. It is odd to reflect that what is in our eyes one of the few just and humane provisions of Spartan society, the right of women to inherit, should have brought about its near extinction, whereas one of the things that saved Athens from a similar fate was the strange and unnatural procedure by which brotherless women were often made to marry their uncles.

THE HOME

The house

No volcano has covered and preserved for us a complete Greek city of classical times in the way that Vesuvius has preserved the Roman cities of Pompeii and Herculaneum, or Thera the Minoan town at Akroteri. However, the town of Olynthus, the capital of a local federation in the north of Greece which flourished from the last quarter of the fifth century until it was destroyed by Philip of Macedon in 348 BC, was the object of American excavation between the two world wars, and a substantial part of a middle-class residential district was uncovered. Though only the foundations of the houses remain, and though nearly all the movable property in them was either destroyed by Philip's soldiers or recovered afterwards by the surviving inhabitants, the evidence from other sources is enough to give us a good picture of the standard Greek town house.

Olynthus was of medium size. Its population, as estimated by its excavators, was about 15,000, some 10,000 to 12,000 being free citizens with their women and children, and the remainder slaves. It was walled, as was usual for cities of the period, and the areas excavated, except where the houses abutted on the city walls, was laid out on a rectangular plan. The streets in the excavated quarter were planned to be 17ft wide, though the main avenue was broadened to 21ft before building began. The blocks were 300ft by 120ft, and each contained ten houses below, notionally 60ft square but in fact marginally less in one

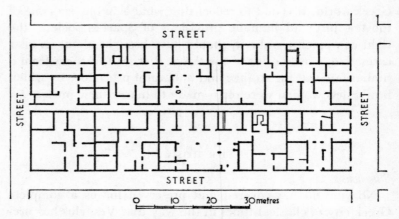

A housing block at Olynthus (*after Robinson and Graham*)

dimension, since there was a tiny lane or gutter between the two rows. The houses facing the main avenue seem to have used their front rooms as shops. In the main avenue stood a fountain house with water piped from the municipal supply.

The material of the house walls was adobe (sun-dried brick), which is cheap, strong, and gives good insulation. Its only drawback is not being able to withstand water. For this reason walls were built on stone foundations. Wood was used for the columns of the inner porticoes, which supported the verandah of the upper storey, the staircase, the joists for the upper storey floors, and the rafters for the tiled roof. The ground floors were normally of pressed earth or clay; those on the first floor may have been so too (the clay being pressed on reeds laid across the joists), or they may have had floorboards. In the bathrooms of the houses cement, slate, or tiles were used for floors, and in the main rooms the floor was often made of cement or a pebble mosaic laid in cement. The inside walls were plastered and painted. There was no window glass, but window openings were equipped with wooden shutters. All the rooms gave on to an open inner portico or on to the courtyard where stood the altar of Zeus Herkeios, the centre of the family's religious observances. No two houses are exactly the same, but p 94 shows a typical ground-plan. The second storey did not necessarily extend all round the courtyard, and indeed the south side was regularly kept to a single storey or to a simple wall in order to allow the winter sun to reach the portico.

In two of the houses inscriptions were found recording the deed of sale together with the price. One was 2,000 drachmae (for an unpretentious and probably single-storied house), and the other 5,300 drachmae (a double-storied corner house with two shops opening on to the main street – the house at the bottom right of the diagram on p 92.

The free-standing house of a richer resident was also excavated at Olynthus. Its plan was much the same, though on a somewhat ampler scale. It had a second dining-room, as did one or two of the houses in the blocks, and a second gate at the back leading to an orchard or garden – a feature familiar to readers of ancient comedy, where a rear entrance is often convenient for the plot.

Not everybody of course lived in town houses of this design. In Athens, at least, multiple residences (apartment houses or tenements), and in the country farmsteads may have followed a different model, the latter having a farmyard wall and a round tower to serve as a barn and byre.

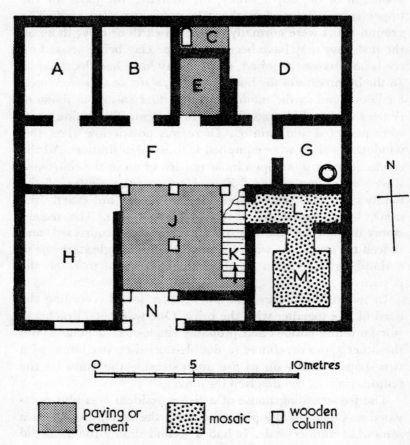

A typical Olynthus house (*after Robinson and Graham*)

A }
B } living rooms
C   bathroom
D   kitchen
E   drying-room behind kitchen
    fire with flue above
F   portico (with verandah
    above)

G   store-room
H   utility room
J   open court
K   stairs to upper storey
L   ante-room
M   dining-room
N   vestibule and
    porch

The furniture

Greek furniture was less varied than ours – no cupboards, wardrobes, display cabinets, or bookcases; no upholstered chairs or sprung beds; no clocks; and of course no electrical fittings, cookers, refrigerators, radios, or television sets. The elaborate furniture (that seen by the guests), consisted of the front door, which belonged to the owner and did not go with the house, and was made resplendent with bronze nail-heads, bronze plates for the keyhole, and an ornate bronze knocker; and the dining-room couches (anything from three to nine in number, but normally five) with ivory inlay and bronze-fitted detachable head-rests. Rectangular tables, but with three legs and low enough to fit under the couches when not in use, and lampstands would be the only other furniture in the dining-room. Elsewhere in the house there would be one or more stout and ornate storage chests, chairs with a curving back-rest and graceful sweep of legs, perhaps a formal upright chair with arms called a *thronos* (the origin of our word 'throne'), stools, further couches or beds upstairs, maybe a wall-shelf or two, and a loom, if one can call that furniture. Articles not in immediate use hung from hooks, and there would be large storage bins or crocks in the kitchen. Colour and richness were given very largely by the soft furnishings – curtains, quilts, cushions, portières.

Domestic routines

In common parlance houses were divided into the men's part and the women's part. In small houses the former meant little more than the dining-room, and the latter the upstairs rooms. Husbands and wives, when they did not sleep together, slept in their own quarters, but the division was mainly designed for strangers to the family. Male visitors, if they were honourable, did not trespass in the women's part of the house, nor female visitors, if they were respectable, in the men's.

In addition to the general running and cleaning of the house the wife's main responsibilities were children, food, and clothing. This meant more than it would today, when clothing is nearly all mass-produced and most food is bought either already cooked or else ready for cooking. However, all but the poorest wives would have the help of a female slave, and the better Olynthus houses seem to have had room for two or three.

Cooking was done on an open hearth in the kitchen, usually with charcoal, which does not give off much smoke. The fumes escaped through a chimney vent running along the top of one of the walls, the area behind the wall being useful as a drying place or, in some houses, as a bathroom. Many of our staple foods were still unknown. There were no potatoes, tomatoes, or maize – all of which came to Europe from America. Cane sugar, though it was already replacing honey in India, was not known in Mediterranean lands till Hellenistic times, and then only as a medicine; nor was there beet sugar, which was an eighteenth-century discovery. Rice too did not come in till after Alexander's conquests, when it was known as Indian cereal. Spinach only reached Europe (from the Far East) in the Middle Ages. There were no globe artichokes, though cultivated thistles did as well; no bananas, no oranges or lemons till late antiquity; no pineapples, peanuts, Brazil nuts, or cashews; and no cola bean, cocoa, coffee, or tea. There was no distillation of spirits for drinking, and beer, though known, was considered barbarous. Vinegar and water or vinegar and milk could be used as non-alcoholic beverages, but the main drink was wine. This was usually mixed with water before drinking, and most wine may have been resinated, as in modern Greece.

Despite the absence of so much we take for granted, the Greek menu still contained a wide variety of meat, fish, fruit, and vegetables, which, often elaborately prepared, embellished the meal, or made it interesting. The foundation was always cereal – wheat or barley – taken either as porridge or as bread. Cooking was done with oil. Butter, though known, was little used, most milk being made into cheese. The day began with a light breakfast, of bread dipped into wine or else some fruit, and the main meals were taken at mid-morning (often in the courtyard of the house) and in the late afternoon.

Formal dinners took place in the men's apartment, and wives did not attend. The diners reclined on couches. In the classical period this was still a fairly recent innovation, for Homeric heroes had sat down to eat, and in Crete, always conservative, men still followed that custom in their communal messes. In Macedonia a man was not allowed to recline until he had proved himself by spearing a free-running wild boar. Respectable women always sat to eat, the only ones that reclined being the sort that were invited to parties – the courtesans or *hetairae*. When the guests had stretched out, tables laden with food were brought in, one for each couch. The wine came in a large bowl, mixed with water at the host's discretion, and was ladled into the diners' own cups. After the meal was over, the tables were taken away, and water was brought in for the guests to wash their hands. They then perfumed themselves, garlanded their heads, the garland being at once the symbol of formality and of the party mood (like dress clothes), and libations were made. These were equivalent to our toasts, though drunk in honour of gods instead of persons or institutions. According to a fifth-century poet, Dionysus and the Graces presided over the first, Dionysus and Aphrodite (the Goddess of Love) over the second, but Quarrels and Disaster over the third. During the final stage of the evening there might be no more than talk or song to accompany the drinking. There could be a game of *kottabos* – flicking wine from the bottom of your cup to try to sink a saucer floating in a bowl of water, or girls might be brought in. If the party was a particularly splendid one, it might end with a cabaret show.

OUT OF DOORS

Men

Unless they were craftsmen or shopkeepers, men of the citizen class did not work regular hours. That smacked of slavery. In theory they did what the season demanded on their farms, and spent the rest of their time doing their job as a citizen –attending the Assembly or the law courts, or carrying out their duty in whatever public office had fallen to their lot. But not all citizens can have been fully occupied in these ways, and we may wonder how they passed their time. They could not spend it at home, for that was a mark of idleness, and the ancient Athenian had no office to shelter in, with files, telephone, and secretary. If he was in business as a merchant, he would meet the people he wanted to meet in the market or at the *deigma*, the great display warehouse at the Piraeus (which was copied in many other Greek harbour towns). Business transactions were conducted largely by word of mouth, good faith and credit being the prerequisites. Contracts of a complicated nature could be written or inscribed on stone. But signatures were not used. Their place was taken by witnesses, who might be asked to accompany the parties to a temple or altar for oaths to be sworn.

These were business occasions. There were social occasions too, either family ones or men-only parties in the evening, and the participants would need to visit the barber's or the perfumier's to prepare for them. Even so, this would not take the whole day. The place a man would most often spend his leisure time was at a gymnasium. There were three large public gymnasia at Athens, all outside the walls – the Lykeion, the Akademia, and the Kynosarges. A gymnasium was a sacred area combining the functions of a public park, a parade ground, and playing fields. It normally included a *palaistra* or wrestling school, baths, a running track, facilities for riding and long jumping, and areas for throwing the javelin and discus. Gymnasia were used by the young for athletic and military training, and by older citizens either for keeping themselves fit or simply watching the young men. Doubtless, like the modern golf course, gymnasia could provide opportunity for business contacts, and in the lively intellectual atmosphere of democratic Athens they inevitably became the scene of much political and philosophic discussion. Just as in English history Lloyd's passed from being the name of a coffee-house to being the name of an association of insurers, so did the name of the Akademia (Academy) and Lykeion (Lyceum, Lycée) pass into the names of the schools of philosophy founded in or near them by Plato and Aristotle. Indeed the word 'school' itself, derived as it is from the Greek *scholē* ('leisure'), is itself a reminder of the Athenian gymnasia as the resorts of spare time.

Women

Until they were safely middle-aged, respectable women never went out except in the company of a female servant. The tabu was a strong one. Theophrastus describes a character who was too mean to buy his wife a servant girl, even out of her own dowry, but who nevertheless hired one for her whenever she had to leave the house. The normal reasons for going out would be to visit neighbours, friends, or relations. Women were not allowed in the gymnasia, and even the theatre seems to have been for men only.

The citizen's wife could only ever really go out for amusement or pleasure on religious occasions. These were the main diversifiers of life in antiquity, as they still are in a Greek village. 'It would be a wonderful place for a festival,' a British traveller before World War I was told by a villager apropos of a possible site for a new chapel on a hill-top. This was in the spirit of the ancient world, where a religious festival was often in one of its aspects a great open-air barbecue. When the animals were sacrificed (as Hesiod's myth about Prometheus explains), the gods were tricked into accepting the bones and fat, while the people ate the meat. The main opportunity that the poor had to eat meat was in fact provided by sacrifices; for meat was expensive. We know from an inscription that the hundred oxen sacrificed at the Great Panathenaea, a major public festival in Athens, in 410 BC cost just over 5,000 drachmae, and that a slightly larger sacrifice at Delos in 375 BC cost 8,000 drachmae, that is 50 and 77 drachmae a beast respectively. There were also sacrifices at the local level, and family sacrifices; and festivals for children, and festivals for women only. We know, thanks to a speech from the law courts, of the wife of one poor citizen, called Euphiletos, who went to one of them with her lover's mother. In comedies when romance, seduction, and an illegitimate baby are needed by the plot, the scene is always a religious festival.

Such festivals were numerous throughout the year, but a woman did not have to wait for one. She might at any time feel the need to visit a shrine or sanctuary. Sostratos, the rich young man in Menander's *Dyskolos*, complains that his mother is for-ever making excursions to sacrifice to some god or other. On the particular occasion of the play she had dreamt about the god Pan, and had hired a professional caterer to go and prepare a large picnic at his sanctuary in the mountains.

Society

Athens was the Paris of the ancient world in being the home of manners, and Attic, like Parisian, was synonymous with the best taste. Speeches from the law courts, Plato's dialogues, comedy, even tragedy, all give us plenty of incidental informa-tion about the practices of good and not-so-good society.

Our most explicit witness is a little book of character sketches by Theophrastus, compactly written in a throw-away style. We are shown how everybody's besetting sin manifests itself in daily life. The characters are easy to recognise and so serve as inter-preters in an unfamiliar world. The compulsive talker ('Excel-lent! And what you say reminds me . . .' is his favourite cut-in phrase) brings us the outdoor life of Athens when he holds up a lesson by chatting to a teacher or athletic coach in the *palaistra* and giving his advice to the boys. The over-anxious man, who always mixes too much wine before his guests come, is also accustomed, like every Athenian, to military service, and asks his superior officer what will be the orders for the day after tomorrow. The unfortunate who can never say the right thing at the right time makes anti-feminist remarks at a wedding, takes a visitor who has just arrived from a distance for a walk, and suggests getting up to dance to a man who is still cold sober. His errors are of course due to ineptitude and he is quite unlike the dreadful man who belches aloud at a tense moment

in the theatre so that everyone turns to look at him, and who
at the barber's or perfumier's declares that he plans to be drunk
that evening. Still worse is the bare-faced robber who feeds his
servant at his host's expense by passing him food from the
dinner table and making a joke of it, who gets into the theatre
free together with his children and their escort on the foreign
visitor's pass that he has applied for on behalf of guests of his,
and who douches himself in the public baths and then refuses
to pay the bath attendant whose job it was to douche him.

Theophrastus gives us thirty of these characters. The one
that gives the best idea of the range as well as the flavour of
Athenian social life is the man who longs for everybody's good
opinion:

> *He hails you from a distance, and says you are just the man he
> wanted to see. After much effusiveness and after embracing you
> with both arms he at last lets you go, only to call you back to
> arrange when he can see you again. If you choose him as an arbi-
> trator he will try to please not only you but also your opponent to
> show how fair he is, and he will always prefer the testimony of a
> foreigner to the testimony of an Athenian. At dinner he will ask to
> see the host's children, and when he does he will at once call them
> replicas of their father, kiss them, and stand them at his side . . .
> He pays frequent visits to the barber, keeps his teeth gleaming
> white, wears good clothes that are never allowed to become worn,
> and makes use of perfume. He is always to be found in the right
> place – in the market, not far from the bankers' tables; in the
> gymnasium, where the ephebes are; and in the theatre, seated near
> the generals.*
>
> *When he buys anything it is never for himself, always for his
> foreign contacts – presents to go to Byzantium, Spartan hounds
> for Cyzicus, Hymettan honey for Rhodes – and he makes sure that
> everybody knows.*
>
> *Naturally he keeps a monkey and Sicilian doves. Naturally too
> his dice are made of gazelle-horn, while his pocket-flasks for oil
> come from Thurii, and his walking-stick with a twist in it from
> Sparta. He has a tapestry embroidered with Persian figures, and*

the courtyard of his house is equipped as a private palaistra and even has a court for ball-games. He publicises his readiness to lend it for philosophers, sophists, fencing-masters, and musicians. But whatever the performance is, he himself always comes in slightly late so that the audience can nudge one another and whisper that he is the owner.

The progress of Greek sculpture: (A) Gravestone of Aristion, marble (c510 BC); (B) Gravestone of a young woman called Hegeso, marble, late fifth century BC; (C) The head of a statue of a young man, bronze, fourth century BC; (D) Portrait head, bronze, c100 BC.

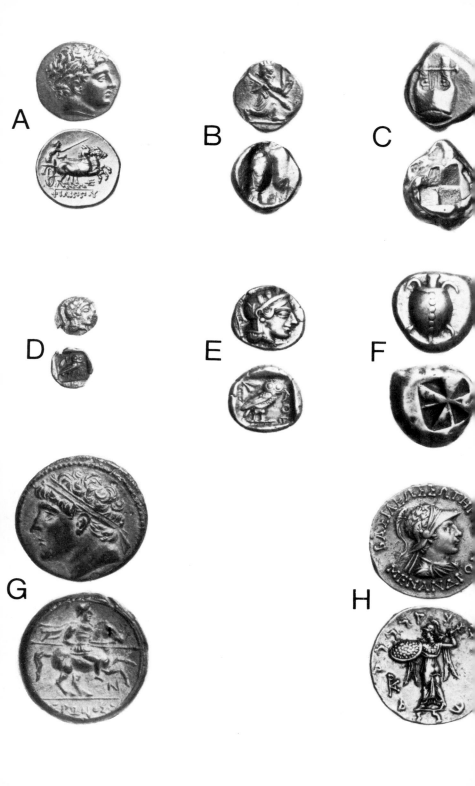

A

B

C

D

E

F

G

H

7

How They Travelled

ON LAND

Personal travel

THE basic means of getting about was by walking, and this remained true to the end of the ancient Greek world. Libanius in the fourth century AD gives us a glimpse of what it was like. Writing of Nicomedia, a city which was subsequently destroyed in an earthquake, he says:

> *Parties of travellers walking from Nicaea to Nicomedia would on the rest of the journey discuss the trees, what were the best crops for the local soil, their families and friends, or literary topics, but when*

———

Greek coins showing obverse above and reverse below:

- (A) Macedonia, Philip II, gold stater
- (B) Persia, gold Daric, fifth century
- (C) Cyzicus, electrum stater, fourth century
- (D) Athens, silver obol, fifth century
- (E) Athens, silver drachma, fifth century
- (F) Aegina, silver didrachm, late sixth century
- (G) Syracuse, Hiero II, bronze
- (H) NW India, Menander, silver
       tetradrachm

they passed the bend in the mountains and the city appeared – and this was at a distance of fifteen miles – when it shone before them, all other conversation stopped, and there was one subject only, the city . . . Whatever their trades, interests, and occupations . . . they were overpowered by the magic of the city's splendour . . . whether they were seeing her for the first time or had grown old in her. One man would point out to his neighbour the palace flashing over the bay, another the theatre shining white over the whole, and others would be explaining the gleams and glints from other buildings, and which was the most splendid was difficult to say. So we would walk towards the city like worshippers towards the statue of their god.

Not only the poor walked and nor were only short distances covered. Galen, the great Greek medical writer of the second century AD, who became physician to the Emperor Marcus Aurelius and whose father was comfortably off, twice walked between Rome and Pergamum in Asia Minor, where he was born. On a smaller scale and in the classical period we hear of people walking the 5 miles from Athens to the Piraeus as an everyday matter, of farmers walking between town and their land in the country, and on one occasion of a deme council meeting in Athens that thinned out during the afternoon when the older members began leaving so as to be back in their village 4 miles away before nightfall.

The rich might ride. The guests at a dinner party in Xenophon's *Symposium* were treated at the end of the evening to a stimulating performance of Dionysus and Ariadne making love to each other, and leaped on to their horses to get home as quickly as possible to their wives. There were horses for hire in Athens. A crippled artisan who used to hire one (presumably to visit his customers) found it an embarrassment to him in a lawsuit in which he was defending his right to draw state aid, since this was granted to the incapacitated only after a means test. He tried to make out that riding was a proof of poverty, for had he been rich, he said, he would have travelled in an *astrabē*. An *astrabē* was therefore some sort of conveyance. Invalids used them, and so did rich men. We once hear of an ostentatious party-lady going to the Piraeus with three donkeys, a donkey driver, three *astrabai* and a retinue of four women attendants. Since we hear of donkeys elsewhere in connection with *astrabai* and never of human bearers, the *astrabē* was probably a donkey-cart that one could lie in, rather than a litter.

Finally, and most expensive of all, was the carriage and pair. Midias, a very rich man, used to drive his wife to the Eleusinian mysteries in one pulled by white mares. Phaenippus, a young aristocrat, sold his cavalry mount and bought himself a carriage, which, according to his adversary-at-law, who tells us the story, was an intolerable affectation for one of his age.

Facilities

For walking and riding all one needs is a beaten track, but for wheeled vehicles there must be a road. Long-distance roads existed, or were thought to exist, in early times – Laius was driving from Thebes to Delphi when he was killed by his son Oedipus, and Telemachus in Homer's *Odyssey* drove from Pylos to Sparta, and both routes go through mountains. Roads certainly existed in the fifth century. Herodotus mentions the road from Athens to Olympia, a distance of 170 miles, and makes a point of the road through the defile at Thermopylae being only single-track, a clear indication that other roads were not. Within Attica we know that there were many roads suitable for vehicles, but in the north of Greece it was only under Archelaus, the king who modernised Macedonia at the end of the fifth century BC, that trunk roads were laid out and built.

In general Greece was, and is, unfavourable for roads. The mountains make them expensive to build and in default of mechanical power laborious to use. The political fragmentation of classical Greece did not help either. Grand networks on the Persian or Roman scale had no place, and the roads that did exist seem for the most part to have been far from grand. On the plains most of them were almost certainly simple dirt roads, and in the mountains, though their construction necessitated both cutting away and building up, the majority were never more than strip roads, with grooves cut smooth for the passage of the wheels but the remainder of the surface left comparatively rough.

Travellers could expect to find watering places along the road, and shops for provisions, restaurants, and hotels in the towns. At sanctuary sites, where there were too many visitors to be absorbed by the town, hotels could be large, double-storied, and built round a courtyard like an eastern khan. We are told by Thucydides that when the Thebans destroyed the town of Plataea in 427 BC, they built such an establishment, 200ft square, beside the temple of Hera, presumably for the pilgrims who could no longer be lodged in the flattened town. A hotel of similar dimensions, which has been excavated, existed at the sanctuary of Asclepius at Epidaurus.

Restaurants and hotels have a poor image in ancient literature, partly perhaps because they did not exist for Homeric heroes, who were always entertained – magnificently – in each other's palaces, and partly because they were a natural target for the jokes of comedians (bad food, bedbugs) and for the disapproval of moralists (rapacious landlords, disreputable company). This poor image doubtless affected the type of person who ran them. Plato, though he admits in theory that shops and inns serve an honourable social purpose, finds himself unable to imagine honourable people running them in practice. Theophrastus, in a character sketch of the man who has lost his sense of position, describes him as the sort who will join in a bawdy dance or become an innkeeper. The ancient world quite lacked our notion of the grand luxury hotel, or even of the comfortable coaching inn. Nevertheless there is no doubt that respectable people of the upper and middle classes did stay at hotels. The merchant in *Menaechmi*, a Roman translation of a Greek play, puts up at a hotel in Epidamnus as if it was the natural thing to do, and in a political speech of Aeschines we hear of ten members of an official delegation staying at hotels along their route.

Transport

Porters existed for carrying personal luggage and handling loads at their destination, but there were no organised gangs of bearers or anything like rickshaw coolies in the ancient Greek world. The two main means of land transport were the pack animal (generally mule or donkey), and the cart (generally ox-drawn).

Two hundredweight would be about a maximum load for a pack animal. A cart drawn by one pair of oxen could certainly take half a ton, and perhaps, though this can be disputed, a ton. Beyond that there had to be multiple yoking. It is evident from surviving buildings that single blocks of stone weighing 10–20 tons could be moved, and surviving inscriptions record teams of from twenty to thirty oxen. We know too from Vitruvius that individual frames were sometimes made to encircle particularly difficult blocks, so that the frame became its own wheel. These were of course special cases. The most special case of all was the *diolkos*, a paved road across the isthmus of Corinth with ruts cut for the wheels of trolleys on which ships could be loaded and hauled to the sea on the other side, presumably by oxen. It dates from the sixth century BC.

A laden ox-cart could in normal circumstances do about 12 miles a day. The cost is less certain, for preserved accounts show great fluctuations. An approximate average for known contracts in the classical period works out at rather under 2 drachmae a ton-mile. This is vastly expensive compared to sea transport. However, there are instances of temples being built close to a source of adequate stone but in fact using a better stone fetched overland from a greater distance. So the cost of land transport, though heavy, was not always an overriding factor.

BY SEA

The ships

Long before the dawn of the classical world seafaring traditions were already ancient in the eastern Mediterranean. The

Minoans from Crete traded at least as far as the island of Lipari north-west of Sicily, and we have representations from as far back as the fourth millennium BC that show galleys with up to thirty oars.

The warship and merchantman of ancient Greece were, as they are today but as they were not in the Middle Ages, quite different vessels. Nevertheless they shared some features. The first was method of construction. Modern shipwrights build a wooden boat frame first, and then cover it with a hull or skin. Greek shipwrights did the opposite. They began with the hull, joining the planks with near cabinet-making precision edge to edge by mortice-and-tenon joints, and added the ribs and frame-pieces later as reinforcement. The outside of the hull was generally sheathed with lead.

Another feature common to warships and merchantmen was the steering mechanism. Instead of a rudder on a post suspended vertically from the centre of the stern, ancient ships had two steering oars slanting down into the water, one from the port and the other from the starboard quarter. Steering was affected by swivelling the oar, there being a tiller bar joined to each steering-oar handle. The two tillers were controlled by a single helmsman. Several ancient authors refer with astonishment to the ease with which one man, by no means necessarily a strong one, could steer a vast ship. The secret lay in the balance of the oar, and the fact that as much blade lay forward of the turning axis as abaft it. The steering oars had some advantages over our single rudder. When docking or when lying to in heavy seas, it was easy to hoist them clear of the water, there was no essential difficulty in repairing or replacing them at sea, and (though there is no evidence that this possibility was exploited) the windward oar could be set at a different level from the leeward.

Another common feature was the square rig. Though lateens were known from the second century BC (and maybe earlier still), the almost universal rig on ancient ships was a rectangular sail hung on a central mast below a single yard. Sheets were attached to the two bottom corners of the sail – the feet in ancient terminology. The yard could be raised or lowered (in strong winds or to escape detection) by means of a halyard running through a block at the top of the mast. Ropes attached at intervals to the lower edge of the sail, and passing up through eyes sewn to the canvas and then over the yard and back to the deck, could be operated to brail the sail in a storm without the need for men to go aloft. Tacking was achieved by swivelling the yard and brailing the forward part of the sail. In this manner an ancient ship could make about one point into the wind.

Classical Greek warships had only this single mast and sail. They used it for cruising and dismantled it before going into action. Merchantmen on the other hand, at least by Hellenistic times, could be threemasters, the mizzen mast and foremast (usually raked forward, half like a bowsprit) having the same rigging as the mainmast. The main could also be equipped with a topsail, which formed a flat triangle between the top of the mast and the tips of the yards.

Anchors were simply 'pierced stones' in Homer's day, and many examples have been recovered by underwater archaeology. The standard classical anchor was invented in the sixth century BC. It had a shank, two arms set at an angle backwards so that one should always be in a position to bite into the sea-bed, and a heavy crossbar (the equivalent of the modern stock) at the top end of the shank to make the anchor lie properly on the bed. Anchors could weigh half a ton or more, and on larger ships were slung from catsheads at the bows and operated by winches or capstans.

The most famous warship of the ancient world was the trireme, the standard fighting ship of the classical period in Greece. It was descended from the pentekonter (see plate, p 68), and first appears at the end of the sixth century. It was long (110–120ft) and narrow (12ft between gunwales, 16ft including outriggers), with a ram prow. It was driven by 170 oarsmen, each pulling his own oar. They were arranged in three tiers, the topmost working on an outrigger which extended the length of the ship. From about the middle of the fifth century the whole was decked in, providing protection for the rowers. There was a solid apron at the prow for the prow officer, and a raised seat at the stern for the helmsman. A fully manned trireme carried ten marines to serve as a boarding party, if occasion called, and four archers. There seems to have been a small number of deckhands in addition to the oarsmen. In command of the ship was the trierarch, the rich citizen who was personally responsible for its maintenance, and he had a second-in-command. The man who needed to be the best seaman was the helmsman, in close liaison with whom worked the prow officer and the *keleustes* ('bo'sun'). The latter transmitted commands to the oarsmen, nursed their energies, and was the person responsible for their training and morale. He was assisted by a flute-player to help the rowers keep time. There was also a full-time carpenter or fitter on board. The full ship's complement was 200.

The oarsmen in the Athenian fleet were paid a drachma a day (half being withheld till the ship paid off in order to discourage desertion and absence without leave!), in addition to a messing allowance of 10 drachmae a month. The team of petty officers who ran the ship, ie the helmsman and his subordinates, was engaged by the trierarch. An ambitious trierarch had to pay over the odds to get the best.

The crew of a trireme, oarsmen as well as petty officers, were citizens, not slaves. In an emergency, when slaves were used at the oar, they were at once given their freedom, so closely did the Athenians identify their navy with their city. In any case a reluctant crew would have been useless. A trireme was a greyhound of the sea, and with so many oarsmen in so confined a space discipline had to be good if the ship was to function at all, supreme if it was to function efficiently. Training was therefore all-important. Regattas and races were frequent. Those held in home waters took place off the Piraeus below the monument which the Athenians built to Themistocles, the founder of their fifth-century navy and the victor of Salamis.

At Salamis (480 BC) the Athenians had 200 ships, not all of them triremes. At the start of the Peloponnesian War (431 BC) they had about 300, of which Thucydides tells us that 250 were at sea in 428 BC. According to the naval lists of 330 BC Athens then had 492 triremes, as well as a few of the larger units that were beginning to become fashionable. The life-expectancy of a trireme was 20 years, so that the average rate of construction for new ships must have been between ten and twenty-five a year. During the fifth century no other single Greek city had a navy half the size of the Athenian, though at the end of it the Peloponnesian allies were able to muster a superior joint fleet and temporarily take away from Athens her command of the sea. She recovered it in the fourth century. After that it was the island of Rhodes and the Hellenistic kingdoms that possessed the great navies of the eastern Mediterranean.

The trireme as a capital ship began to lose its pride of place during the fourth century, and was finally relegated to being a vessel of second rank. It was displaced first by quadriremes and quinqueremes ('fours' and 'fives'), and in the third century these were succeeded by real battleships, 'sixes', 'sevens', and thereafter in accelerating pace up to 'sixteens'. The Ptolemies even built a 'twenty', two 'thirties', and finally, under Ptolemy IV, the largest warship of the ancient world, a 'forty'. It was a failure as a warship, sluggish and unsteady according to Plutarch. Its vital statistics, which have been reported to us, serve to show what was just beyond the practical limits of ancient technology. None the less they are impressive. It was 420ft long, and required 400 officers and men, as well as 4,000 oarsmen. Like the other great warships of the period, it was intended as a floating platform for soldiers and artillery, not an instrument for ramming as the trireme had been. It therefore carried the large number of 2,850 marines.

The arrangement of oarsmen on this and the other large ships of the time presents a problem. Triremes ('threes') certainly had three banks of oars, but whether the 'fours' and 'fives' that succeeded them had four or five banks is less certain. It is generally thought that the number must now refer to the number of men at an oar. Even so there is a limit. Eight or ten men is the maximum that can be deployed on a single oar. Moreover it is hard to see how a single ship of those times could have carried the numbers attributed to it. But these big ships are described to us as being 'twin-prowed', and as having two helmsmen and four steering oars. Reluctant though one is to imagine anything so bizarre, they must have been giant catamarans.

In any case they were too clumsy to last. By Roman times sizes had shrunk again. At the Battle of Actium Octavian's fleet of 'sixes' defeated the Graeco-Egyptian fleet of Antony and Cleopatra, which was largely composed of 'tens', and in the Empire the Roman fleet reverted to a form of trireme, with only one 'six' to serve as the admiral's flagship.

Just as the oar-driven warships became larger during the course of Greek history, so did the merchant sailing vessels. In the classical period the average for a large freighter seems to have been around 130 tons burden, but in the Hellenistic period it was about twice that; and, as with warships, there were some giants built. The largest we know of, about 1,800 tons, was built by Hiero II of Syracuse with the help of Archimedes, the famous mathematician and engineer. It was partly a grain carrier, partly a liner. It had thirty cabins (each of 'four-couch size'), all with mosaic floors, as well as a captain's suite; and further accommodation included a gymnasium, a promenade deck with pot-grown vine and ivy for awning, a small chapel (to Aphrodite), a library and reading-room, baths, and stabling for horses. There was also less luxurious passenger accommodation. The fresh-water tank forward held 20,000 gallons, and there was a salt-water tank for keeping fresh fish. The ship was also armed against raiders – eight towers manned by four marines and two archers each, and an artillery platform with an Archimedes-designed *ballista* capable of shooting a stone or javelin 200yd. The ship successfully completed its first voyage to Alexandria, but we do not know its subsequent history. It was not quite alone in the super-freighter class, for we know of two or three other ships that reached some 1,300 tons burden, and of imperial yachts that approached or exceeded it in luxury of appointment.

Between warship and bulk-carrier there was a range of intermediate types. We know some half a dozen names (*akatos, lembos, keles, kybaia, kerkouros, phaselos*) for merchant galleys using both oar and sail. Each presumably represented a different solution to the demands of speed and manoeuvrability (best satisfied by oars) and cargo space and range (best satisfied by sail), but the evidence is not always enough to distinguish them. Moreover, the words sometimes changed their meaning. For instance, the *lembos* of classical times was the dinghy towed behind the ship (still a Mediterranean practice), but in Hellenistic times the word meant a naval auxiliary vessel that could carry cargo and was powered by anything up to fifty oars. Other types, like the *phaselos* ('bean' – a fast passenger boat) had a short life, being attested only in the literature of the first centuries BC and AD.

Passengers and cargo

Two figures of the first century AD give us an idea of the number of passengers carried in an ancient ship. There were 276 persons on board when St Paul was shipwrecked off Crete, and 600 on the ship Josephus took from Palestine to Rome. A large *phaselos* is mentioned by Sallust (first century BC) as carrying a whole cohort, and a cohort numbered 600 men. We have no figures for the archaic and classical periods, but the smaller ships of those times would certainly have carried fewer passengers.

Except perhaps for some short-haul ferries, there were no specialised passenger services and no regular timetables. To make a voyage meant waiting for an opportunity. Nevertheless from a busy port like the Piraeus there were probably frequent enough departures for most normal destinations during the sailing season (winter sailing was avoided as far as possible). We often hear in speeches from the Athenian law courts of passengers taking ship at short notice. With favourable winds an ancient ship could expect to make an average of 4 to 6 knots (100 to 150 miles a day), and with adverse winds half this or less. Of course storms could introduce whole days of delay, as well as considerable danger. Another danger was piracy, which, as in the modern world, was prevalent in some periods, rare or absent in others (see plate, p 68). Insurance was unknown, but for ship-owners its place was largely taken by a system of bottomry loans. These were raised on the ship and its cargo, and were only repayable if the voyage was successfully completed. We hear of rates as high as 100 per cent, but the average rates charged in fourth-century Athens – 30 per cent to the Crimea, 12 per cent to the Bosporus (minimum sailing times of 21 and 10 days there and back respectively) – do not suggest a very high assessment of risk.

Cargoes might be anything from sacks of almonds (in the Kyrenia wreck off Cyprus, about 300 BC) to Egyptian obelisks (the Vatican obelisk weighs 322 tons and was transported to Rome together with four pedestal blocks of 174 tons, and 800 tons of lentils as ballast – a cargo of 1,300 tons – on a specially built ship which was afterwards put on display and was eventually filled with concrete and sunk to form part of Claudius's new harbour at Ostia). The main trade from Athens was to grain ports on the Black Sea, and in later antiquity the grain imported by Rome from Egypt alone totalled 150,000 tons a year. Wine, carried in pottery amphoras, was perhaps the second most important single commodity. We hear in Athenian law cases of large cargoes of hides, of wool, of dried fish, and of timber. The recent science of underwater archaeology can add an unexpected variety, including looted bronze statues, millstones, marble capitals, and even, from early Christian times, a carved and ready-to-assemble church pulpit.

8

How They Learned

In the third century BC a Cynic philosopher called Teles described the educational experience with professional gloom:

> *Infancy is full of frustration. When we are hungry our nurse puts us to bed, when we are thirsty she gives us a bath, and when we want to sleep she shakes a rattle at us. No sooner are we free of her clutches when we fall into those of the escort, the coach, the teacher, the music-master, and the painting-instructor. Arithmetic, geometry, and riding-lessons lie in wait for us. Early to rise is a rule. Rest is forbidden. At last we leave boyhood behind. Yet our exit from it is only an entry into another world of terror – the marshal, the trainer, the fencing-master, the Governor of the Gymnasium. We have been whipped and watched and ordered about all our lives, and we are already twenty . . .*

After this bad beginning, he continues, life grows worse still, as is proved by the fact that when we reach the age of prosperity, public office, and tax-paying, we all praise our boyhood as the happiest years of our life!

Another description, given by Aristotle a hundred years before, is more serious and systematic. Education is divided into categories of subject, and the utility of each is stated. In tabular form this is what Aristotle's scheme would look like:

Category	Use
Literacy	Business; management of one's private affairs; the acquisition of information; general purposes of public life
Gymnastic	Health, strength, and courage
Music	Leisure (which is more fundamental than work, since leisure is what we work for)
To which some add design	The ability to purchase well; the appreciation of physical beauty

It is surprising to see gymnastic and music in this select list. The reason is an historical one. Greek education, which was to finish up in the dry embrace of the grammar school, began its institutional life as a sort of combination of singing lessons and athletic coaching.

ARCHAIC AND CLASSICAL EDUCATION

Gymnastic

The standard Greek argument for gymnastic education was that it turned out strong healthy warriors. It is not very convincing, and it did not convince the thoughtful. It was already being attacked by Xenophanes in the sixth century BC, and in the fifth a character in Euripides scornfully asks whether soldiers throw the discus or expel invaders by wrestling with them. Even the claim that hard physical training was good for the health was disputed by ancient medical writers. However, the argument was probably irrelevant. From the actual syllabus pursued in ancient gymnastic education it is clear that its real aim was neither health nor war but sport. Everything in it was subservient to the cultivation of excellence in the five athletic events (foot-race, long jump, discus, javelin, wrestling, boxing) which formed the recognised basic programme at the Olympic and other public festival games. As we have already seen, these games were of considerable antiquity and had a favourable public image. Athletics had been the sport of the Homeric hero, and most of those who contested in the games were young men of wealth or aristocratic family. Victory was not only the peak of personal ambition, but also brought pride and glory to one's city.

It is easy to see that in these circumstances there would arise a demand for coaching, and ultimately for professional coaching. The demand was being met by 500 BC. The vase-painting illustrated in the plate on p 68 shows a pupil being instructed in the long jump by such a coach (*paidotribes*, boy-trainer. This is one of the coach's earliest appearances on the scene of Greek education, and he was to remain a key figure in it for centuries.

Music

The other key figure was the music-master (*kitharistes*, lyrist). Later educational orthodoxy regarded his job as the shaping of the soul, just as the coach's job was the shaping of the body, but we may wonder whether in this case also the moral argument was not contrived later to justify an existing habit. For here too there was an aristocratic image. Singing to his own accompaniment on the lyre was one of the accomplishments of the Homeric hero, and the ability to pass the lyre properly at after-dinner drinking parties and to sing to it was as much a symptom of good breeding in archaic and classical Greece as knowing that port should be passed to the left is alleged to be in English life.

Another function of the music school was to provide choruses for the great religious festivals, and Plato takes it for granted that not to have been trained for a chorus is the same as not having been educated. Here again the aristocratic ambience is manifest. To sing to the lyre, to join in the choir, and to compete in athletic sports were activities expected of the *jeunesse dorée* of early Greece; so it was as natural for them to require music-masters as it was to require athletic coaches.

Reading and writing

It is not known when reading and writing, which were destined eventually to become almost synonymous with education, first entered the syllabus. The Greek alphabet began to be used in the eighth century BC, and vase-paintings show us writing lessons in progress in Athenian schools at the end of the sixth century. So somewhere between these dates the subject was introduced into the curriculum, and that is all we can say for sure. Moreover in other parts of Greece it may have been introduced later than at Athens, and in the backward-looking societies of Sparta and Crete, where the educational system did not develop as it did elsewhere, writing may have had a much less important place in children's upbringing.

Another problem is who taught writing in the schools. The Greek word for writing-master (*grammatistes*) does not appear in Greek literature until the latter part of the fifth century BC. So who taught the alphabet before that? There are some reasons for thinking it was the music-master. A comic account of old-fashioned education written in 423 BC implies that the lyrist and the coach were the only types of teacher, and the same account tells us that the lyrist taught not only how to sing but also what. He made his boys learn poetry. This is confirmed by early vase-paintings that show the music-master making his boys use a written text. So he could obviously read and write. We may even speculate further. Though there were no professional scribes in archaic Greece, there was a class of persons for whom writing was a professional accomplishment, and this was the poets, who were by necessity lyrists and choir-masters. So poet and music-master may well have been essentially the same profession, overlapping each other in much the same way as do the modern professions of scientist and university teacher. The poetess Sappho, we know, kept a sort of training college for young ladies in Lesbos, and on several Athenian red-figure vases of around 500 BC the music school is shown as the scene not only of the learning of poetry but also of the alphabet (see plate, p 85). Lessons are being given in the double flute and in writing while the escort (*paidagogos*) of one of the boys watches. On the wall behind is the school equipment – a papyrus scroll, writing tablets, a lyre, and a ruler in the form of a setsquare. The date is 490–485 BC.

The size of schools at this time can be roughly guessed at

from the only two figures we have, both recorded as the result of disasters. There were over a hundred children at a school in Chios in 496 BC when the roof fell in, killing them; and a man went mad and killed sixty children at a school in Astypalaia in 492 BC.

Moral upbringing

The coach and the music-master gave technical instruction. The escort, though he doubtless gave plenty of advice, was a family slave. How then did a boy pick up the social and ethical values of his own class? He would have absorbed a great deal in the way of traditional history and traditional values from his learning of the poets, but their application to contemporary reality would have needed something more positive. The gap was filled by a custom that strikes us as strange. An older boy was expected to form an emotional attachment to a man of mature years. The relationship was frankly homosexual – the Greek words for the participants mean 'lover' and 'beloved' – and doubtless found physical expression often enough. But in principle this was frowned on. The idea was hero-worship on the one side and tutelage on the other. The boy accompanied the older man to the gymnasium and to drinking parties, learning from his conversation, his example, and his songs. The ethos of upper-class society was largely transmitted through such party songs and verses. 'I tell you', sang Theognis to his protégé Cyrnus, 'what right-thinking men told me when I was your age', and the advice he passes on in this way, though poetic enough in its setting, consists largely of prosaic social tips such as the proper attitude to adopt towards money, the importance of choosing friends from one's own class, and the dangers of populist politics.

HELLENISTIC EDUCATION

Learning to read

The rapid increase in the number of books after the end of

H

the fifth century BC forced schools to devote increasingly more attention to literature. Eventually there emerged a new pattern of education, broadly standard throughout the Greek world.

A papyrus instruction manual of the third century discovered in Egypt in 1935, many fragments of school exercises found in Egypt and elsewhere, and the remarks of ancient educationists like Quintilian enable us to reconstruct the routine syllabus taught by the writing-master. Thoroughness was its hallmark. After learning the names and shapes of the letters, the child was taught every possible combination in which they might be used. First came the seventeen consonants of the Greek alphabet followed by each of the seven Greek vowels – as it were ba, bĕ, bē, bi, bŏ, bu, bō; ga, ge, gē, gi . . . and so on. Then the order was was reversed – ab, ĕb . . . ag, ĕg . . . etc. Next the open syllables were repeated, this time each being followed by the letter n (ban, bĕn etc). This order was then reversed (nab, nĕb etc). Closed syllables like bab, bĕb, gag, gĕg, followed, and after this closed syllables with consonant clusters like zros and zrus, combinations which hardly ever occur in practice. Then came the numerical use of the alphabet, for one Greek way of writing numbers was by using the letters, as if we were to write a = 1, b = 2, and so on to j = 10, ja = 11 . . . k = 20, ka = 21 etc. At last the pupil was introduced to words themselves, first to monosyllabic ones (especially those that were difficult to pronounce, like *lynx*), then to words of two, three, four, and five syllables. Finally verse passages in various metres for reading or dictation exercises were introduced and some more arithmetic (such as the square numbers and how to write the fractions of the drachma), and at last this stiff initial training in the use of the elements (which is the same in Greek as the word for letters) was concluded. We do not know at what age the teaching of them normally started, or how long it took.

Literature

In the study of literature poetry still took first place in

Hellenistic times, though it no longer held a monopoly. The most frequently read school authors were Homer for epic, Euripides for tragedy, Menander for comedy, and in prose Thucydides as a historian and Demosthenes as an orator. Many other authors were read in these genres and in others, and the range was further increased by the use of selections and anthologies.

Teaching methods and objectives seem to have been generally agreed on. The schoolmaster's first duty was to make sure he had a good text of his author. Today with printed books we take this largely for granted, but then it necessitated personal checking. The second step was to show how the text should be read. This again was not as straightforward as it would be now, for written literary texts had begun by being in the nature of an author's prompt-copy, and they still bore the signs of their origin. There was no division between words, no regular punctuation, and in the text of plays, though there was a sign to indicate when the speaker changed, the names of the characters speaking were not written in. The ancient reader, therefore, had to do more work than the modern one, and he had to learn how to do it. It was an important stage, marked by the fact that reading competitions between schoolchildren were organised on public occasions. After reading came exegesis, the explanation and interpretation of the text. The final task, and the professed purpose of the whole process, though it is not clear how it was carried out in practice, was judgement, or literary appreciation.

Literary education was given to girls as well as boys, and we even possess a portrait of a literature mistress (see plate, p 86).

School organisation
The ancient world had no certificate examinations, and though team games existed, they were not taken anything like as seriously as they are today. But then as now schools needed a target for pupils to aim at and a visible testimony of success to set before parents and patrons. One thing they did in this

respect was to be represented at religious festivals, entering choirs for the music competition and individuals for the athletic events. Another was to organise displays of their own. We have a long inscription from Teos, a city on the Asia Minor coast, which lists three sets of competitions for three age-groups. Common to all three are reading aloud and an otherwise unknown event called *hypobolē*, probably a form of recitation. There was only one other event for the oldest group, 'responses', which sounds as if it might have been capping verses like the modern Cretan *rhizetika*. The middle age-groups had competitions in painting and in general knowledge, the youngest in handwriting, the harp, the lyre, singing to the lyre, and five items called 'the torch' – 'rhythm', 'comedy', 'tragedy' and 'lyric' – though quite what they implied is not easy to say.

The Teos inscription shows clearly the increasing concentration on literature. It also reveals one noticeable drop-out from the musical scene – the flute – mainly because (and there is other evidence of its decline) it had apparently now become a professional instrument instead of an amateur one. On the other hand the lyre, which kept its place in the schools, had been discarded by professional musicians. The contrast is significant of the attitudes and objectives of Hellenistic education.

We know something about the financial side of Hellenistic schools, thanks mainly to the discovery of two second-century BC inscriptions, one from Teos again and the other from Miletus. The former records the generosity of a certain Polythrous, who donated 34,000 drachmae for the education of all freeborn citizens, boys and girls. This sum was to be the capital of an endowment fund to be administered by the city, and it was to pay for the following staff:

3 writing-masters	at 600, 550, 500 dr pa	
2 coaches	at 500 dr each pa	
1 harpist or lyrist	at 700 dr pa	
1 fencing-master	at 300 dr for a minimum contract of two months	Posts to be reconfirmed annually
1 archery and javelin instructor	at 250 dr for a minimum contract of two months	

The other inscription records the donation of 10 talents by a benefactor called Eudemus to pay for four writing-masters at 40 drachmae and four coaches at 30 drachmae each per month. Unfortunately we do not know the number of pupils at either school, so we cannot calculate the staff-student ratios. Nor do we know what fees were paid by parents in the two cities before the generosity of Polythrous and Eudemus relieved them of the burden.

Further education

The subjects most frequently studied by those who wanted to continue their education were rhetoric and philosophy. The educationist's standard justification for the pre-eminence of these subjects was that speech and reason were the most specifically human of all accomplishments. But there were also more worldly reasons. There was the image of the Homeric hero, who was characterised for his skill in debate at least as much as for his courage in battle. There was practical utility, because before the invention of printing and before the introduction of cheap paper the spoken word played an even greater role in communications than it does now. There was also historical tradition, for the enlightenment of the classical period had been diffused by the speeches and public debates of travelling experts, the so-called sophists. Some of these had offered explanations of the world, others the techniques necessary to master it by mastering the art of persuasion. In all but the most backward fifth-century cities a man's effectiveness depended much more on his ability to put an argument across than on his birth or his money. So ambitious young men had made it their business to attend the sophists, quite apart from the excitement of their verbal witchcraft or radical ideas.

Eventually what had begun as a series of opportunities for intellectual stimulation became routine, and institutions were established. For instance, Isocrates opened a school of rhetoric in Athens around 390 BC, having previously had one in Chios. A few years later Plato began regular teaching at the Akademia gymnasium, and in the next two or three generations other schools of philosophy were founded in Athens by Aristotle, Epicurus, and Zeno. These schools made Athens a permanent centre of higher education, though it was not the only one. Alexandria, Pergamum, Rhodes, all achieved international fame as places of learning. Others had more local reputations, but no city was altogether deprived. The tradition of the travelling philosopher or rhetorician never died out – indeed numerically the travellers may have remained in the majority – and the visit of one of them to a small city could be quite a local occasion. They were in fact one of the mechanisms, like the touring companies of actors and like travelling craftsmen generally, by which the cultural unity of the Hellenistic world was maintained.

Further education might be pursued to various lengths. At its slightest it could be just a year spent listening to lectures on subjects from astronomy to painting – a sort of foundation year or liberal arts course. A full training in rhetoric would take much longer. The subject expanded, as subjects do in the modern academic world, to meet the prestige in which it was held. Different styles were prescribed for different classes of speech, such as non-controversial speeches of occasion, debating speeches, and speeches in a law court. Different styles too were recommended for different parts of a speech, such as introductions, conclusions, argument, and narrative. Special training was devoted to the cultivation of memory, to the art of organising one's material, and to the art of thinking it up in the first place. There were practical exercises in which voice and gesture were not neglected, and unpractical exercises in which pupils were asked to make up speeches for highly spiced situations (such as what Alexander said on finding that he had run out of countries to conquer, or the arguments a would-be suicide could use if he wanted to sue his rescuer for saving him), and when they had delivered their speeches and been criticised they would then listen to the master's fair copies.

Such were some of the items in the rhetoric syllabus. The main alternative was philosophy, which did not promise wordly success but the understanding of truth and consequent personal happiness. To the serious and persevering student each of the schools could provide a universal and coherent philosophy, but we may guess that such students were in the minority, and that most would pick and choose. The Academy was interested primarily in mathematics, the Lyceum (Aristotle's school) in natural science, while the Garden and the Stoa (the schools of Epicurus and Zeno) were concerned first and foremost with systems of personal morality. The schools experienced declines and revivals, but their differences and the element of competition between them ensured a vigorous intellectual life throughout Hellenistic times and for long after.

Subjects not in the educational mainstream perpetuated themselves in basically the same way as crafts did, by a good student attaching himself to a master. So there is little to say about them except what they were and how they were likely to be regarded by a young man choosing his career. A fairly representative list is given by the physician Galen in a sort of recruiting manifesto for the medical profession. In the first circle of the élite and secure (whom he sees well-bred and well-groomed clustering round Hermes, the God of Speech and Reason) he places geometers, mathematicians, philosophers, physicians, and astronomers; in the second circle painters, sculptors, schoolteachers, woodworkers, builders, and stone-cutters; and in the third circle all other craftsmen.

We must make allowance for Galen's own position. He was both a Platonist and a physician. The one will have inclined him to put geometry first and to leave out rhetoric altogether, the other to raise the position of medicine. We can be sure that most Greeks would have put it in the second circle. But otherwise the list is a fair sample of how the professions, arts, and crafts stood in the orthodox Greek educational hierarchy.

9

How They Improved Their World

THE MEANING OF IMPROVEMENT

'OUR sciences are entirely Greek', wrote Francis Bacon in 1610, 'and the contributions of the Romans, the Arabs, and of more recent times have been few and derivative.' He goes on to say that unfortunately 'Greek philosophy was scholastic and disputatious', and that when it began, 'useful inventions stopped'. Bacon's points were revived with characteristic élan by Macaulay in his magnificent essay on Bacon, published in 1837. If forced to choose between the first shoemaker and a philosopher like Seneca, who wrote three books 'On Anger', says Macaulay, he would choose the shoemaker. 'It may be worse to be angry than to be wet. But shoes have kept millions from being wet; and we doubt whether Seneca ever kept any-body from being angry.'

Bacon and Macaulay confined their attack to ancient philo-sophy (or to be more precise ancient philosophy from Plato onwards), but the issue has been generalised in more modern times by those who take the Marxist line. To them ancient philosophy was not a prime mover but a symptom. The real malaise was the class structure of ancient society, especially its division between masters and slaves. The ruling classes were the mind of society, the ruled its body, and the function of philosophy was to preach to the ruling classes the comfortable message that they were the only ones that mattered. This analysis is tempting since it seems to explain a number of different things in a single stroke. But there are difficulties with it. People in antiquity were just as keen on making money as people are now, and it is hard to imagine them intentionally refraining from inventing new techniques that would have allowed them to do so. A more important objection to the Marxist explanation is that it begs the question. It assumes that technology and industry both stagnated and that Graeco-Roman civilisation represents a sort of plateau in the ascent of humanity with steeper gradients both before and after. Though it is impossible to draw a definite graph of a vague concept like the rate of material progress, when one looks at the list of Greek discoveries and considers the tremendous increases in scale between the beginning and end of antiquity, stagnation is hardly the word that springs to mind.

It remains true that ancient philosophy by and large did condemn preoccupation with material welfare. No longer, though, does this seem such a spoil-sport or reactionary attitude as it did. With the present rate of increase of human consumption it has become much clearer to us than it was in the Renaissance or in the Industrial Revolution that mankind cannot aim at unlimited physical expansion. We shall do better therefore to exercise modesty and to judge the Greeks, if we must judge them, by their own rules rather than by those of the nineteenth or twentieth century.

An idea of what the average Greek thought that human civilisation was about is not to be got by quoting individual moralists or philosophers. A better guide for us will be the popular 'lists of inventors'. Greek literature of all levels and all periods is full of references to the man who was the first to do this or that for the benefit of humanity. The list of benefactions includes the discovery of the basic agricultural crops – corn, grape, and olive – and also the main crafts, or industries as we would call them, such as the introduction of fire, with its consequences for pottery and metal-working; the invention of carpentry, ship-building and chariot manufacture; and the development of writing, weights and measures, and counting. More surprisingly it includes what we would call social innovations – music, religious rites and festivals, written laws, and more particular innovations like military ranks and military discipline, games, coinage, beacon signals, and even mealtimes! The common factor, explicitly stated by more than one fifth-century author, is the transition from a haphazard cave-dwelling animal-like existence to a life of order, security, and comparative ease.

TECHNICAL AND SCIENTIFIC DISCOVERIES

Primary production

The domestication of the olive seems to have taken place in Crete in the Early Bronze Age. Apart from this Greece cannot claim the credit for any significant discoveries in the way of new foods, though many were introduced (mainly from the east) and passed on (mainly to the west). There was some improvement in cultivation. For instance, Theophrastus in the fourth century BC knew of only two varieties of apple, but Pliny in the first century AD of thirty-six. The most dramatic and important improvement made by the Greeks in the realm of food production, however, was undoubtedly in the processing of cereals. Raw grain takes a great deal of time and energy to eat and digest, to say nothing of wear on the teeth. It is a much more efficient food source if it is first pulverised into flour. In Neolithic times, throughout the Bronze Age, and still in archaic Greece this was done by rubbing the grain between two stones, one of which was held in the hand. Two minor improvements in the system seem to have then been introduced. One was the cutting of grooves or striations into the rubbing surfaces of the two stones. The other was the conversion of the top stone into a hopper, by hollowing it out so that it could hold a quantity of grain, and cutting a slit through it so that the grain fell through on to the lower stone. The next, and most important, step was taken before the end of the sixth century. This was to fit the upper stone on a wooden bar hinged at one end, mount the whole on a table with the lower stone let in at the edge, and then with the other end of the bar to push and pull the upper stone over the lower. This push-pull mill, with its greatly increased ease and speed of operation, became standard and remained in use until at least the end of the third century BC.

It was then to be superseded. Every visitor to Pompeii is struck by the bakeries with their great circular mills – cone-shaped lower stones surmounted by upper stones in the shape of hour-glasses pierced for wooden bars to go through. Over a hundred of them have been found in this medium-sized town, and they were turned by donkeys. The donkey-mill seems to have been invented (perhaps in Italy and not in Greece) at the beginning of the second century BC, as was a smaller-scale version which worked on the same principle but was turned by hand. These two forms of rotary mill, the one more productive and the other more portable, between them ousted the push-pull type.

Finally, at some time during the Hellenistic period, an even more impressive grinding machine was invented – the water-mill. It is mentioned by three writers of the first century BC. Vitruvius explains the principles of its construction, Strabo mentions the presence of one in Asia Minor, and a writer of a poem in the *Greek Anthology* plays with the notion that, now the river nymphs can do the hard work, the golden age will come again for mankind. It was quite a long time in coming. Rome does not seem to have had water-mills on a large scale until the third or fourth centuries AD, and was not dependent on them till the fifth or sixth. However it did come, and the water-mill is perhaps the most important single legacy of a technological nature which the ancient world bequeathed to the medieval.

It has been calculated that a Vitruvian type water-mill could grind 150–300kg an hour as compared to 25–30kg in a donkey-mill, and 4–5kg by the original saddle-quern. This is a massive improvement in performance, at least comparable to the development of the large grain-carrying ships of the Hellenistic and Roman worlds.

The principle of gearing, which made the water-mill possible, was also employed in Greek Egypt for irrigation. The *sakkiyeh*, the bucket-chain driven by an animal walking round and round which is still a common sight in Egypt, seems to have been introduced in the second century BC. It was preceded by the Archimedes screw (also used for draining mines). Both devices enabled much larger areas to be irrigated for very much less expenditure of work than the earlier *shaduf* or swing-balance, which had been known since at least the third millennium BC. They were later supplemented by the vast *noria*, or water-wheel, which is first attested in Egypt in the second century AD, and which subsequently spread to Morocco in the west and to Japan in the east, reaching there in AD 800.

Arms and armour

The expansion of the Greek world between 800 BC and 200 BC was largely due to the superiority of Greek military equipment. In the archaic period the main innovation was the hoplite army, which consisted of heavily armoured infantry fighting in closed ranks. Though it could not be effective without good training and morale (Aristotle dated the beginning of Greek democracy to the appearance of the hoplite), its basis was the armour of beaten bronze worn (and owned) by each independent citizen soldier. The key item was the shield. It was comparatively small (3ft in diameter) and light, being made of wood with bronze plating, but its effectiveness and originality lay in its double handle (a bronze rail across the centre through which the left forearm passed) and a leather thong at the inside of the far rim which could be gripped by the left hand. The shield could therefore be held rigid or let go (thus freeing the hand for other uses without losing the shield). Above the shield was a bronze helmet, which covered the whole head, including the neck, cheeks, and nose, and was beaten from a single sheet of bronze, no easy feat. Inside it was a lining to make it soft enough to wear. Below the shield were bronze greaves, closely tailored to the leg so that they would clip on. The body itself was covered, in the earlier period, with bronze plates, front and back. Later this was found too heavy and replaced with a linen corselet on to which scales of bronze could be sewn.

A complete suite of armour might include ankle-pieces, thigh-guards, shoulder-pieces, and arm-pieces, but the total protection of the medieval knight was never aimed at. The success of the hoplite concept is shown not only by its having remained paramount in Greece throughout the archaic and classical periods, but in the victories won by Greek hoplite armies against foreign forces, and the employment of Greek hoplite mercenaries by foreign potentates.

The second major invention of Greek military technology was the trireme, which we are told was developed by Corinth in the sixth century BC. The trireme's advantage was speed. The only measure of performance we have is from Xenophon, who says that the voyage from Byzantium to Herakleia on the Black Sea coast (140 miles) took a long day. This must imply a maintained speed of some 10 knots, which is good going for a rowing boat at sea. Unfortunately we have no data to tell us how much better the trireme was than its predecessors.

The third great Greek military invention was artillery. The best long-range weapon in Homer's day, and indeed until the end of the fifth century, was the composite bow, which was made of three layers – wood in the middle with sinew glued on the front and pieces of animal horn on the rear. When the bow was drawn taut, the sinew was stretched, the horn compressed. The maximum accurate range of the weapon seems to have been 150 to 200yd. There was no technical objection to building more powerful bows. The limiting factor was the power of the archer to string it. Odysseus, in Homer's *Odyssey*, could be recognised because he was the only person strong enough to set up his own bow.

The first attempt to overcome this limiting factor was made by the artificers of Dionysius, the ruler of Syracuse, in 399 BC. The result, called a 'belly-bow', was a composite bow mounted on a central shaft. It was successfully employed in the siege of Motya in 397 BC, where it is said to have been a novelty and to have surprised the Carthaginians. Its range then was perhaps 250yd. Later models mounted on a fixed base with a swivel joint and operated by means of a winch were in use by the middle of the century. We know of one type that could fire an arrow or bolt 6ft long and 1½in in diameter, and another 'mountain model' for bolts 4ft long. Their range was perhaps 300yd.

This seems to have been the limit using the principle of the bow. Experiments soon began to be conducted for producing a mechanical sling or catapult for hurling stones, powered by animal sinew or by twisted hair. Such machines were in operation as early as 340 BC, when the Athenians seem to have captured some at Eretria. Thereafter catapults are listed in the Athenian official inventories. Philip of Macedon played a large part in the development of catapults, and his son, Alexander the Great, made much use of them in his campaigns, notably in his siege of Tyre.

After this, machines for firing bolts and for hurling cannon-balls both counted as indispendable military equipment. The extent of their use in Hellenistic times can be suggested by a few figures. In 227 BC after the great earthquake of Rhodes (the one that destroyed the Colossus) Hiero II of Syracuse, who wished to see Rhodes' power restored as quickly as possible, sent the city fifty catapults and 20 tons of hair. Rhodes itself, 7 years later, sent 8 tons of hair and 2 tons of sinew as aid to the city of Sinope on the Black Sea coast. In the west, when the Roman general Scipio captured New Carthage in Spain in 209 BC, he took 476 catapults; and when Carthage itself fell to the Romans in 146 BC, it was found to contain 2,000 catapults. Round stone cannonballs have been found in great numbers at various ancient sites. Their weights vary, but cluster round averages of 40, 12, and 7kg, suggesting three standard sizes of machine. Artillery was regular equipment on Hellenistic war-ships.

On land its primary use was in seige warfare. For defence the catapults were mounted in gun-rooms inside the towers of a city wall. The engineer's problem was to design the towers and their embrasures so that the whole area in front of the wall could be covered. He endeavoured to keep enemy catapults out of range by constructing earthworks outside the walls. The besieger on the other hand could use movable siege-towers to increase his range. In particular he might try to demolish the parapets above the walls with his stone-throwing catapults and then, with his bolt-shooting machines keep the walls clear of defenders while he advanced his storming party. Accuracy was essential for the success of this tactic, and there is evidence that ancient artillery was accurate even against individuals for ranges up to 300–400yd.

The size of buildings

Greek buildings, especially their public ones like the temples, are generally thought of in terms of their beauty. The care taken over the stone used, over the refinements of proportion, over decorative details such as column capitals, and over architectural sculpture show that their beauty was not an accidental effect, and the pride that the Greeks took in it is manifest in many literary texts. However, from the aesthetic point of view early buildings can often be more attractive than later ones, and it is easier to talk of taste as changing than as improving. But where there was unquestionable improvement in Greek building was in the matter of scale, especially internal scale. Brute size presented no particular problem. The Parthenon (about 440 BC) is massive enough, 160ft × 65ft, and the naval arsenal at the Piraeus (about 335 BC) was even bigger, 434ft × 59ft. But inside they consisted, like a modern church, of a nave and two aisles, the naves having a width of 25ft and 21½ft respectively. This narrowness was not from choice. Twenty-five feet is the largest practicable length for a wooden beam, and this had always been the limit. Neither Xerxes nor Rameses, nor any king of the more distant past, however resplendent, had ever sat in a room with more than this amount of clear space in it. There then had to be a column to hold up the roof. The first breakthrough came with the invention of the trussed roof, which enabled the span to be nearly doubled. The council chambers at Priene and Miletus, both about 200 BC, each attained clear spaces of about 45ft. The next breakthrough came with the arch, and its companions the vault and the dome. The arch had been introduced into the Greek world in Hellenistic times, but it was first used on a major scale in Roman public buildings, baths and basilicas, where we find internal widths approaching 100ft. The Pantheon of AD 120 is as much as 147ft across. This, however, was a round building. The final step came with the discovery of how to put a dome on a square, and the crown of late Greek architecture, the church of St Sophia built by Justinian in Constantinople, has an uncluttered inside space of 220ft × 107ft under a great central dome and two half-domes at each end, large enough to accommodate the whole Parthenon with plenty of room left over.

The fine arts

Here again it is normal to look at Greek art from an aesthetic point of view, where there can only be talk of change, not of improvement. In the technical sphere, however, where they can be certainly identified as such, improvements abounded. We have seen that even in so ancient and well established a craft as pottery the Greeks invented the multiple brush attached to a compass for drawing concentric circles in the Dark Age, and this invention, though trifling enough in itself, was adopted as far afield as Carthage in the eighth century BC and the south of France in the sixth. Athenian potters invented new and ingenious shapes for specific purposes, such as a wine-cooler and a child's chamber-pot. There were also new media. The use of mosaic, first pebbles then tesserae, dates from the end of the fifth century. Glass was introduced from Egypt or Syria in classical times, and glass-blowing (which made the material cheap and universal) was invented in the Hellenistic period, though perhaps not by Greeks.

Beyond question, however, the most important artistic innovation was the discovery of how to draw in perspective. Virtually all proper Greek painting, executed on wood or plaster, has disappeared, but its trends are reflected in its humbler cousin, vase-painting, from which it is evident that the art of perspective drawing was evolved during the fifth century BC. Ancient perspective differs from modern perspective (of which the rules were worked out during the Renaissance) by not assuming a single point of vision, and it has been plausibly conjectured that it originated in scene painting for theatrical productions. However that may be, it enabled the artist to draw the human body from any angle and in any posture, to place individuals in a group in relation with each other, and to draw furniture, buildings, and landscapes in a convincing manner. The difference can be easily appreciated by comparing Minoan or Egyptian wall-painting with the frescoes and mosaics of Pompeii and elsewhere, which, though Roman in execution, are Greek in inspiration and, many of them, direct copies of Greek originals.

Other innovations

Other innovations of varying importance include chairs with arms, cupboards, window-panes of glass up to 200cm × 300cm and greenhouses (though these may be specifically Roman), the fluked anchor, the lateen rig, the gear-wheel, the screw, the multiple block or pulley and the cranes that it made possible, the water-organ (the predecessor of our church organs), and the water-clock.

This last sheds a particularly vivid light on the ethos of Greek invention. Though the sundial was known from the middle of the fifth century BC (it is said to have been introduced from Babylon by Anaximander), the normal way to tell the time in classical Athens was by pacing one's shadow. But in the law courts, where it was thought essential to give both sides an equal period of time to state their case, a stone jug with a hole at the bottom was used to allow a measured amount of water out at a measured rate. The same principle could obviously have been used to discover the approximate time of day. The difficulty was that the Greek hour varied its length according to the season of year, the twelve hours being counted from sunrise to sunset.

I

We do not know who first tried to make a clock. One ancient tradition credited Plato with the invention, and Aristotle is said to have had an alarm clock which was set going the night before and which woke him up by dropping a bronze ball into a bowl. If it existed, it was presumably water-operated. But whatever the truth of these stories it seems certain that in the middle of the third century BC Ctesibius of Alexandria invented a water-clock which not only marked but sounded the hours. What the public saw was the statue of a boy pointing a wand at a column on which were inscribed lines for each hour; beside the boy was the statue of a trumpeter. As the day passed, the boy with the wand rose slowly up the column (because he was attached to a float in the water-tank below) and at each hour the trumpet sounded (because a gearing mechanism, also worked by the float, dropped a bronze cloche down a pipe into another tank of water, and the air in the cloche was forced up the pipe and blew the trumpet). Adjusting the tap that let the water in to the main tank each day when the clock was reset would have taken care of the varying length of the hour, and a missing cog in the driving gear could have allowed the cloche or compressor to drop every hour and then to be slowly wound up again during the next hour. However, the description of the clock by the Roman engineer Vitruvius is not altogether clear, and these may not have been the exact means adopted.

The first public town water-clock that we hear about, though almost certainly not the first to have existed, was set up in Rome in the forum in 139 BC next to the public sundial there (first set up in 263 BC). The still-standing 'Tower of the Winds' in Athens was a water-clock of the first century BC. Another, we do not know when or where it was built but it may have been already old, is commemorated in a poem in the *Greek Anthology* by Antiphilus of Byzantium (first century AD):

> *My twelve divisions trace the hidden sun,*
> *Twelve times sound passes through my tongueless throat,*
> *When, water-squeezed, the air is forced to run*
> *Up a tight tube and play a trumpet note.*

A public clock, by Athenaeus made,
I tell the time of day, come sun or shade.

By this time water-clocks may have been quite common. The rumbustious millionaire Trimalchio, in a novel by the Roman writer Petronius, had one. Lucian (second century AD), describing Baths designed by the Greek architect Hippias, mentions that they contained a water-clock with a sounding device. Procopius in the sixth century described an elaborate town clock in Gaza with the twelve labours of Heracles to represent the twelve hours. A clock of the same period presented to Gundibald, King of Burgundy, had Diomedes blowing a trumpet, a bronze snake hissing, and model birds twittering – miracles to a barbarian, says the surviving description of it, but commonplace to us. These ancient clocks are the direct ancestors of the elaborate medieval public clocks that still survive in many European cities. It is evident from the ancient descriptions we possess of them that they were admired equally for their ingenuity, their appearance, and their usefulness.

Mathematics and science

The cardinal discovery of Greek mathematics was that numbers cannot do everything. For instance, whatever number of units of length you call the side of a square you cannot accurately state the length of the diagonal of that square using the same unit: the two are incommensurate, or to put it another way the square root of 2 is an irrational number. The same applies to circles. The circumference is always the diameter multiplied by a figure slightly less than $3\frac{1}{7}$ and slightly more than $3\frac{10}{71}$, what we call π. You can perhaps express the ratio more closely, but you can never express it exactly. This strange and disturbing discovery cannot in its very nature be proved empirically. It demands an abstract geometrical exposition, and Greek mathematics always remained abstract, geometric, and demonstrative. For all that, many of the theorems it evolved were of great practical use, eg in calculating the dimensions of spheres and cones, in ballistics and surveying, and in astronomy.

Astronomy led to one of the most important innovations made by Greek mathematicians – the science of trigonometry (or *chords* as they called it). Its own most impressive discovery was that of the precession of the equinoxes, the slow wobble of the earth's axis, which takes some 26,000 years to complete. It was made by Hipparchus (born c190 BC) by comparing his own star map of over 850 stars with the Babylonian records, to which he had access. Hipparchus also discovered the length of the year to be 1/300 of a day shorter than 365¼ days, a result not incorporated into the European calendar until 1582, by Pope Gregory XIII (and not accepted in England till the eighteenth century). Another impressive discovery, made before Hipparchus, was the size of the earth, which was generally accepted as being spherical. The calculation is deceptively easy. Syene (Assuan) is on the tropic, and the midsummer sun is exactly overhead there at midday. Measure how far off it is from being overhead at Alexandria. The circumference of the earth may then be found by simple multiplication (Fig 7).

If Syene is 5,000 stades (about 500 miles) south of Alexandria, and the angle you have measured is 1/50 of a circle, then the earth's circumference will be 250,000 stades (about 25,000 miles). The calculation is by Eratosthenes (born c275 BC), and

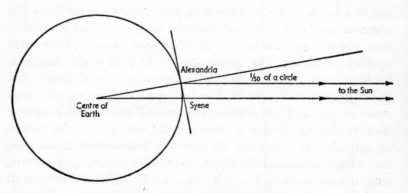

Finding the circumference of the earth

comes very close to the truth, though the use of round numbers suggests that he was interested in a theoretical demonstration rather than in a surveyor's accuracy. Indeed to the Greeks in their limited area of the world the precise dimensions could not be of any great practical utility.

Finally, any account of Greek astronomy must mention the famous theory of Aristarchus of Samos (born c310 BC) that the sun, not the earth, was in the centre of the universe. His theory was known to Copernicus, who championed it, but it was not generally accepted in the ancient world. There was in fact nothing in either observation or theory which compelled its acceptance. Greek instruments were not accurate enough to detect the parallax of the nearest fixed stars (the different angles subtended by them when the earth is at opposite extremes of its orbit round the sun), and though the movements of the planets look neater and more symmetrical on the view that the sun is in the centre, this is counterbalanced by the greater awkwardness of explaining gravity. On the standard Aristotelian view, the centre of the earth was the same as the centre of the universe, and the natural movement of all bodies with weight was towards this one centre. On the Aristarchan view no such neat explanation of weight was available.

Discoveries in other fields included the octave and the whole system of expressing concordant intervals by simple numerical ratios (eg the fifth by 3:2, the fourth by 4:3); the fact that air was a substance and its presence necessary for the transmission of sound; laws of reflection and refraction of light; the sciences of statics and hydrostatics; many refinements in anatomy and surgery; and in physiology the existence of the nerves and the function of the brain as the centre of perception and voluntary motion. Less dramatic but no less important than new discoveries was the mass of information collected and transmitted in encyclopaedic works associated with the names of Aristotle (mostly in zoology), Theophrastus and Dioscurides in botany, Euclid in mathematics, Ptolemy in astronomy, Hippocrates and and Galen in medicine. Unfortunately in later antiquity and the Middle Ages, when circumstances were less propitious for independent scientific inquiry, these collections came to be looked on as final authorities, and thereafter some of the reputation for being stagnant which should rightly be confined to those who did not improve on these compilations has rubbed off on to the compilers themselves, giving Greek science as a whole an undeservedly static image. In truth, however, as this brief list of its achievements may show, there was as much enterprise in this as in any other aspect of Greek life.

IMPROVEMENTS IN SOCIAL ORGANISATION

Many of our everyday routines, some of which seem so obvious that we never think of them as needing to be invented, are Greek in origin. The simplest and most ordinary of all perhaps is arranging things in alphabetical order. Yet though there was a standard order of letters in the Greek alphabet (and in its predecessor, the Phoenician, at least as early as the fourteenth century BC), the alphabetisation of entries in a list was first done in the third century BC, probably in Alexandria, and then at first only for initial letters. Counting votes in a secret ballot seems another obvious procedure, but it was probably done for the first time in the Athenian law courts. Written receipts date only from Hellenistic times. Another innovation of the highest importance, whose results are with us still, was coined money (see plate on p 104). It was not strictly a Greek invention, being credited to Lydia, a state neighbouring the Greeks in Asia Minor, but its universal diffusion is certainly due to the Greek cities of the sixth century BC. The routines of public relaxation, the gymnasium, the palaistra, and the baths on the one hand, athletic competitions and festivals on the other, deserve to be included in a list of Greek innovations that improved the quality of life. There are also the forms of entertainment which began as children of these festivals – public displays of epic poetry, drama, even history and philosophy, all of which were later transmitted through the medium of books, thanks to the unrestricted literacy of the Greek world.

The habit of the book was adopted by the Romans, and, given new life in the Renaissance by the invention of printing, has been with us ever since. Redolent of the recluse as it is and often dusty, the book is a strange legacy from the free and open air of ancient Greece. But without it there would not have been any other.

10

What Has Survived from Ancient Greece

LANGUAGE

Words

THE Greek that is spoken in Greece today has survived in unbroken tradition from ancient Greece, though there have been great changes in pronunciation, grammar, and vocabulary, and a modern Greek cannot read ancient texts without some special training. Ancient Greek also survives in the languages of modern Europe, including our own. English is by heredity a Germanic language, but only about a third of its basic words are of Germanic origin. Nearly half are Latin, borrowed either directly or through French, and most of the remaining sixth are Greek. Foremost among these are the technical terms of science, medicine, and philosophy, but they also include a great number of everyday words –the *air* we breathe, the *butter* we eat, the *place* we occupy, even the *daffodils* and *squirrels* of our countryside. Many Greek words entered the stream of western European vocabulary in early Roman times – *scene, pain, pirate, anchor, sponge, chest, chart, sack,* to cite only a few. Others came in when Rome had already annexed most of Greece – for example, *grammar, syllable, allegory, ideal, cube, leopard, cyclic, chair.* More again were brought with the diffusion of Christianity – Christ (which is the Greek for 'anointed'), *baptism, church, bishop, monk, priest, deacon,* and so on. There are in all over 1,100 such Greek words that have come into our language through Latin. Another large number have been either taken over by modern languages directly from Greek (eg *atheist, automatic, climax, cosmetic, episode, erotic*) or coined from Greek roots to describe new inventions and discoveries (eg *antiseptic, dynamo, ecology, stereophonic*). These words, which are revivals rather than survivals, form a large category, well over a thousand in normal use, and more than twice that if one includes the more recondite scientific and medical terms.

Words of Greek descent, therefore, make up a significant part of our language. But that is not all. An equally important class of words is modelled on Greek though using native roots. For example, our Latin-derived 'conscience', the German 'Gewissen', and the Russian 'soznanie' are all compounded from words meaning 'know' and prepositions meaning 'together' and are all modelled ultimately on the Greek *syn-eidesis*. Similarly 'quality' and 'quantity' come to us from the Latin translations (*qualitas* and *quantitas*) of the Greek *poiotēs* and *posotēs* ('what-sort-ness' and 'how-much-ness'). In fact the Romans quite consciously created much of their language in this way, and we are their heirs. So we have 'civil' (Latin *civilis*, Greek *politikos*, which has also given us 'politics' by direct borrowing), 'essence' (Latin *essentia*, Greek *ousia*), 'substance' (Latin *substantia*, Greek *hypostasis*), 'refer' (Latin *refero*, Greek *anaphero*), 'case' (Latin *casus*, Greek *ptōsis*), 'continuous' (Latin *continuus*, Greek *synechēs*), and hundreds of similar words. The fabric of our language is shot through with translated Greek terminology of this nature, quite apart from the substantial percentage of our vocabulary that is already Greek in origin.

Metaphors, phrases, and proverbs

Pompous metaphors like 'the ship of state' and fossilised Latin phrases like *a fortiori* and *deus ex machina* derive from Greek, and it does not surprise us to be told so. But there are also a large number of quite homely phrases that one would never suspect of Greek birth if one did not trace their pedigree – phrases like 'trusting one's own eyes', 'cutting the knot', 'having two anchors out', 'handing on the torch', 'a sea of troubles', 'second childhood', 'with one voice', 'kicking against the pricks'. Some of them have come to us in continuous descent through Latin, others were revived by Renaissance books of proverbs, and a few are of more recent introduction. For instance, 'haves' and 'have-nots' and 'working capital', which are first quoted in English dictionaries from 1836 and 1912, are straight translations from Greek political and financial language.

By no means all the Greek proverbs that have been introduced into English have become fully naturalised. 'Look to the end', 'nothing to excess', 'know thyself' still, after several hundred years' use in English, sound like texts for sermons rather than the small change of conversation. Even 'having a wolf by the ears' is a trifle exotic. The real test of a fully accepted proverb is when you do not need to say it all: 'Many a slip . . .' and 'Birds of a feather . . .' are at once understood even if '. . . 'twixt cup and lip' and '. . . flock together' remain unspoken. 'Well begun . . .' automatically implies '. . . half done'. Yet these are all Greek proverbs. What has made them so at home in English is the rhyme. This often took a long time to discover. The translation of the Greek proverb that literally means 'like to like, jackdaw to jackdaw' made by Wyatt in 1525 ('each thing seeketh its semblable') does not run trippingly off the tongue. The next attempt was less clumsy, 'like will to like' (Heywood, 1546); and the cement of the modern rhyme was first found in a play of 1578 by George Whetstone – 'byrds of a fether, best flye together'. Other proverbs have the same history. The rhyme of 'slip' and 'lip' is not quoted before the nineteenth century, nor the rhyme of 'begun' and 'done', though the proverbs themselves were taken over in less arresting form in the sixteenth century. Other Greek proverbs put into modern dress include 'coals to Newcastle' ('owls to Athens'), 'out of the frying-pan into the fire' ('from the smoke to the flame'), 'one swallow does not make a summer' ('. . . spring').

Finally there are allusions. 'Hyperion to a satyr,' said Shakespeare's Hamlet, seeking the most vivid way of contrasting grace with turpitude. 'O Attic shape' exclaimed Keats of his Grecian urn, summarising in the one word all the qualities of natural good taste which were in his time considered characteristic of Athenians. We continue the custom when we call somebody a 'sybarite' or an 'Atlas' or a 'Cassandra', and when we describe friendships as 'Platonic', attitudes as 'stoic', replies as 'laconic', or conditions as 'Spartan'. Each of these words is a window on the ancient Greek world.

LITERATURE

Means of survival

A great deal of ancient Greek literature survives in Greek. Though it is only a portion of what once existed, it represents on the whole what succeeding generations of scholars and teachers have thought most worth keeping. The way it has survived has been by constant recopying, first on papyrus rolls, then (from the early centuries of our own era) into books of papyrus, vellum, or paper (this last was introduced from the east in Byzantine times), and finally (since the Renaissance) into print. A few works have survived only in Latin or Arabic translations. A few more, and fragments of many others, have been recovered from ancient papyri found in excavations, nearly all from the dry climate of Egypt. Inscriptions of a literary nature have also been found. But for the overwhelming majority of what we have we must thank the ancient and Byzantine copyists.

Before 500 BC

The characteristics of archaic Greek literature are that it is all in verse and that it was all composed for delivery aloud. In the early part of the period (though this is a matter on which we have no direct evidence and on which opinions differ) works may not have been written down till long after they were composed. But however and whenever it was committed to writing there is no doubt that the fountainhead of archaic Greek poetry, indeed of all Greek literature, is Homeric epic. The two long epic poems which are attributed by Greek tradition to Homer and which survive in the entirety are the *Iliad* and the *Odyssey*. They are both in hexameter metre. This is roughly equivalent to English blank verse, though the line is dactylic, not iambic; it operates according to a pattern of heavy and light syllables, not a pattern of stress or accent, and the line structure itself is richer and rather more disciplined. Both poems have a coherently organised plot set in a clearly imagined heroic past. For example, the weapons are of bronze, not of iron, and the heroes ride in chariots, not on horseback. This is similar to the Wild West where there are pistols but no machine-guns, railroads but no bicycles. But there are differences as well as similarities. The world of the Wild West has few fixed placenames and is little more than a detailed stage setting for exciting things to happen in. The Greek heroic world on the other hand centred on actual places, known characters, and important events. Some of the places were small and unimportant in Homer's time (probably around 700 BC), but major capitals in the Bronze Age and this makes the tradition look genuine. If so, the personal names may be historical too and the key events, like the Fall of Troy, may have happened somewhat in the way they were remembered. Homer's strength as the source of Greek literature, however, does not depend on the truth of the historical scenario, but on the skill with which he integrated his story into it.

The *Iliad* embraces the whole story of the Greek war against Troy, telling us how it started and allowing us to see how it will end, and in doing so introduces us to a remarkably full spectrum of different characters. But though this is its theme the action of the poem takes only a few weeks and deals directly with just a single climax – the duel between Achilles and Hector in the last year of the war. Even more surprising in a war poem than this unity of subject is the sympathy with which it sees sadness in the ultimate fall of the enemy city of Troy and in the plight of Achilles, the star of the Greek warriors, who finds that the supreme glory to which he has dedicated his life turns to ashes when he has won it.

The *Iliad* is thus a prototype tragedy, whereas the *Odyssey* is essentially a romance, or, as Aristotle called it, a comedy of manners. After recounting the manifold adventures that befell Odysseus on his way home from Troy and making clear the crisis confronting him when he found that his palace was occupied by his wife's suitors, it ends happily with him recovering both his wife and his palace with the aid of his only son, Telemachus.

Homer was succeeded by several other poets who composed stories of the heroic past, filling out the various gaps they considered Homer to have left in telling the story of Troy, or dealing with other areas of legend, such as the war against Thebes or the life of Heracles. Their work only survives in occasional quotations in later writers. In the same tradition of narrative epic verse are the shorter 'Homeric Hymns' – festival pieces in honour of particular gods, composed for the most part as overtures to full-length recitations of epic.

Quite different from the glories, adventures, and splendour of Homer, though composed in the same metre and according to tradition at the same time, was another form of epic, which aimed at supplying information rather than excitement. The two surviving works of this school are attributed to Hesiod, a Boeotian farmer of pessimistic turn of mind. They are quite short, each of about 1,000 lines, and are known as the *Theogony* and the *Works and Days*. The first tells how the gods came into being and who they all are, and the second gives practical advice on farming and on everyday life.

Homer and Hesiod comprise most of the poetry that we possess from the archaic period. It was by no means all the poetry that was written. This was the lyric age of Greece. There were songs for choirs, songs for individuals to sing to the lyre, drinking songs, love songs, hate songs, marching songs, even political manifestoes and satires. Their authors include some of the most famous names of Greece: Sappho and Alcaeus, Archilochus, Solon, Tyrtaeus, Anacreon, and others. It was they who invented nearly all the metres that were to serve the poetry of later antiquity. Enough of their work survives to let us see how wide and varied the world of Greek literature already was and how many different human moods could be at home in it. Even so, it is a pitifully small amount. Much of it is fragmentary or in the form of quotations, and there are few complete poems.

500–300 BC

Epic poetry continued to be composed in the classical period. Indeed its range was extended and Choerilus of Samos put contemporary history into epic dress. His work does not survive, but we do have some of its literary descendants in Roman historical epic. Lyric poetry continued also, and the best-known writer of choral songs, Pindar, belongs to the fifth century. We have four books of his 'victory odes', written for patrons who won events in the Greek festival games, to perpetuate the pride of the moment. They still have an astonishing power to lift the clouds even for readers today, when many of the things that Pindar valued most – birth, breeding, money, physical beauty, and athletic prowess – are out of intellectual fashion. Even so, the chief renown of classical literature does not lie here. It lies in two new fields, drama and written prose.

The Greek drama we have is all Athenian. Its origin lay in a form of choral song in which the choir acted a story with impersonations. Its occasion was, as so often, a religious festival in which rival choirs competed for a prize. Gradually it came to be felt desirable to have individual parts impersonated by individual actors; but competitions need rules, and the number of actors allowed was rigidly laid down. First one, then two (the innovation is ascribed to Aeschylus, but we do not know how he won acceptance for it), and finally three. There were never more, just as we never exceed the number laid down for a side at football or at tennis. The rule did not limit the number of characters in a play. All it meant was that there could never be more than three on stage talking at the same time, since there were only three actors available to take their parts. The acting of different characters by the same actor was made easier by the convention that actors wore masks.

The only three writers of tragedy whose plays survive are Aeschylus, Sophocles, and Euripides. We have seven each of the first two, and eighteen of Euripides', together with further fragments from ancient quotations and papyrus discoveries. The plays that have survived intact represent a conscious selection made in later antiquity, and are only two or three per cent of the tragedies that must have been written and produced during the century or so in which the form flourished. In essence a tragedy was no more than the serious retelling of a story from the past (nearly always the heroic past) by means of impersonation, but in practice it became the main medium of artistic communication in the Athenian democracy. In addition to the dramatic excitement that could be got from the skilful handling of the stories, helped by the occasion and the large open-air audience (10,000 or more), the conflicts between the heroic characters could easily be made relevant to the political issues of the day, in particular the instincts of human nature versus the requirements of social order, and the level of debate adjusted to take account of the new wisdom and new ideas being introduced by the sophists.

Comedy, in its fully institutionalised form, dates from the latter half of the fifth century, and was modelled on tragedy. But whereas tragedy took an allegedly real event and tried to make it plausible in contemporary terms, comedy set out from an absurd idea. In one women take over the Assembly, in another they organise a sex strike on an international scale to get their husbands to stop making war, and another shows the foundation of a utopia in the clouds to be financed by a transit tax on sacrifices from earth to heaven. The nearest an English reader can come to the spirit of these plays is to imagine the richness of Gilbert and Sullivan combined with the outspokenness of *Private Eye* – for comedy's tongue was as free as its fantasy.

All that the Middle Ages has spared us of Greek comedy is eleven plays of a single writer, Aristophanes. However, we do have twenty-seven Latin plays adapted or translated from later Greek comedy – called New Comedy to distinguish it from the Old or Aristophanic type. This was pale and prudish in comparison, and its themes were domestic, not social or political. Its most famous exponent was Menander (342–290 BC), and though later Greek critics spoke of him in the manner we reserve for Shakespeare ('Real life or Menander – which copied which?'), none of his plays survived the Middle Ages. In recent years, however, one virtually complete play and substantial fragments of others have been found in papyri from Egypt.

The writing of history began in the late sixth century, but the two earliest historians whose works have survived lived at the end of the fifth century. Herodotus took for his subject the whole history of the civilised world, culminating in the Persian Wars between the Greeks and the Barbarians, Thucydides a study in contemporary history, the Peloponnesian War between Sparta and Athens and their respective allies. Their styles are as distinct as their subjects, the former discursive and personal, the latter compressed and objective. Herodotus published his work by public readings, Thucydides perhaps by private ones. We cannot tell if the works of either circulated in private copies, though it was the end of the fifth century that first saw books for public sale.

Lectures on philosophy, politics, literary criticism, and such subjects were certainly composed and given and probably circulated in written form in the fifth century, but we only possess fragments of them. The first philosophers we have in bulk, Plato and Aristotle, wrote in the fourth century. They are again opposites in literary style, the one lively, speculative, and exciting, the other terse, commonsensical, and comprehensive. Two writers of the second class from this period also survive in quantity – Xenophon, mainly a historian, and Isocrates who wrote mostly on educational, philosophical, and political subjects.

An unexpected survival from fourth century prose is oratory – law-court speeches and political addresses. They were pre-

served, especially those of Demosthenes, as classic examples of
the art of speaking in Hellenistic times, when the acquisition
of eloquence had become the prime goal of education.

After 300 BC

Almost all classical literature had been meant for oral delivery. Hellenistic literature on the other hand was more often
composed for the reader, though it seems that throughout
antiquity readers, even when reading to themselves, spoke the
words aloud. New Comedy survived for a while into this period,
but otherwise dramatic productions were either of classical plays
revived or sub-literary. Poetry continued to be written, as one
would expect, and there was even an original school of it – the
Alexandrians, or 'moderns' as they could be called. However,
the main originality of Hellenistic literature was its scholarship.
There were several centres of learning, Rhodes and Alexandria
being the most famous. Alexandria had its famous Library,
founded and maintained by the Ptolemies. Collections of
authors and commentaries on them, essays in criticism, manuals
of rhetoric and other technical accomplishments, scientific and
medical treatises, glossaries, and catalogues were produced in
Hellenistic times, and eventually came great encyclopaedic
compilations. But 'the ancients' were always present to the
mind of later Greek literary men, and old genres might always
be revived. There was even a revival of life style in the second
century AD, when Greek intellectuals travelled from city to city
giving public lectures (and as far as we can tell finding en-
thusiastic audiences) in the manner of the sophists of 600 years
before. On a lower level there were writers of exceedingly
romantic novels, and a substantial sub-literature offering a
range of goods from magic to religious consolation. There was
also the literature of the young Christian church – the New
Testament, lives of saints, and the writings of the early fathers –
and this was in time destined to become the most widely read
Greek literature of all.

K

ART

Sculpture

The main materials of Greek sculpture were marble and bronze. Since both are of value when melted down, the one for its lime, the other for its metal, very little original Greek sculpture (see plate, p 103) has been continuously visible since antiquity. The first time that ancient statues were unearthed in quantity was in Italy during the Renaissance, but most of them were either Roman or Roman copies of Greek originals. Their numbers were increased with the excavation of Pompeii and Herculaneum in the eighteenth century.

Already in the seventeenth century travellers in Greek lands had begun finding original Greek sculpture. Their aim, understandably enough, was to send back what they could to their own countries, where the statues could be both safe and seen. The most famous such collection in the English world is the architectural sculpture from the Parthenon, sent to London at great personal expense by Lord Elgin at the beginning of the nineteenth century. Elgin aroused the wrath of Byron, who called him 'the last, dull, spoiler', and now that Greece, Turkey, and the other countries of the eastern Mediterranean have emerged as modern states, Byron's view that antiquities should be left where they are has become standard. The result is that the distribution of Greek sculpture today is less logical than it might be. Outside the eastern Mediterranean the collections are better or worse according to the prosperity that different countries enjoyed in the eighteenth and nineteenth centuries; in Greek lands they reflect mainly what happens to have been found in the more recent excavations. Luckily, however, modern techniques of illustration have done much to remedy this inconvenience, and there are many representative histories of the whole of Greek sculpture assembled between the covers of books.

The crafts of ancient stonecutting and ancient sculpture did not survive in any major way in the Greek world. Byzantine churches are brick-built and Orthodox dogma disapproved of representations of saints in the round. These factors did not apply in the west. Here the stonemason and carver continued to exercise their crafts throughout the Middle Ages until the time of the Renaissance and the revival of classicism. Taste then took a great leap into the past, and has since then continued to move backwards in line with archaeological discovery. Baroque took for its inspiration the grandiose and ultra-realistic sculpture and the elaborate ornament of Roman and late Hellenistic times. One of the most admired pieces was the large Laocoön group, a father and his two sons being squeezed to an agonising death by two sea-serpents. It was carved by Rhodian sculptors about 25 BC, highly praised by the elder Pliny, a Roman writer of 100 years later, rediscovered in 1506, and universally admired once more from then until at least 1766, the date of Lessing's famous essay on it. But with the Greek revival of the late eighteenth century, admiration was transferred to the serenity and balance of the classical art of the fifth and fourth centuries BC and to its imitations by Canova and Thorwaldsen. Nowadays it is more fashionable to admire – as indeed Plato did – the freshness and nobility of archaic sculpture, the most important examples of which have only been discovered in the last 100 years.

Painting

The only original Greek painting of the archaic and classical periods, apart from a few fragments, survives on pottery. The best and most famous is from Athens, in two main styles. In the black-figure style (from about 625 BC) the figures are painted: in the red-figure style (from about 525 BC until about 330) the background is painted and the figures left in the natural red of the clay (see plates, pp 68 and 85). An exceedingly high standard was attained in both styles, and Athenian pottery occupies one of the peaks in the history of human art, though a peak in a minor range. Luckily we possess many thousands of pieces, and examples are to be found in most important museums throughout the world. They therefore give the most accessible as well as the most immediate contact with the spirit of ancient Greece.

The objects themselves are of course only cups, jugs, and bowls of comparatively low worth in their day. They are scarcely mentioned in Greek literature, and were in fact not even recognised as Greek until the middle of the eighteenth century. Until then they were either unnoticed or passed as Etruscan, since almost all of them came from Italian graves. This is why Josiah Wedgwood, the English pottery manu-facturer, christened his factory 'Etruria' in 1769. So great was the artistic importance attributed to them that the British parliament of the day voted £8,400 to buy a collection to sti-mulate the manufacture of British pottery and to help raise its standards of design.

Full-scale painting (murals or wooden panels) was a prestige art from the fifth century on. We know the names of the great painters of the classical period – Polygnotus, Apollodorus, Zeuxis, Parrhasius, Pamphilus, Pausias, Apelles – but we have no works of theirs, only a few accounts of what they did and some stories about them. One of the taller stories is that of a challenge match between Zeuxis and Parrhasius. Zeuxis exhi-bited a painting of grapes; and birds came down to peck at them. When Parrhasius produced his picture, Zeuxis asked if he might unveil it. But when he went to draw the curtain, it was not there. The curtain was the picture. So Zeuxis acknow-ledged defeat since he had deceived only birds but his rival had deceived him! These stories underline what we would in any case gather from other evidence that a main aim of fifth-century painting was to perfect techniques of realism, including perspective and the mixing of colours.

To compensate for our total loss of original Greek painting we possess much Roman painting and many Roman copies of Greek painting, some as frescoes and some as mosaics. They were first found at Rome in the Renaissance, but the best examples come from Pompeii and Herculaneum and the sur-rounding villas, and are to be seen either *in situ* or in the Naples

Museum. The crafts both of mosaic and of mural painting survived through the Middle Ages, Constantinople fostering the best work.

Other arts

Imposing ruins of ancient Greek architecture have always been visible in southern Italy, Sicily, Greece, and Asia Minor – mainly temples and theatres. Few civic buildings and domestic houses have survived, apart from foundations and ground floors recovered in recent excavations.

For the minor arts survival has depended first and foremost on durability of materials. Wood and textiles do not last in Mediterranean countries outside Egypt, so we have hardly any furniture, clothing, carpets, or curtains. Silver and gold do last if they are not stolen, so we have a great many coins. They are small and easily lost, and might also be purposely hidden away in hoards by owners who for one reason or another never got back to recover them. We have also a fair amount of ancient jewellery, but rather less plate, which is bigger and less easily lost or hidden. The plate we do have comes mainly from graves.

In all these arts, as with sculpture and painting, there has been not only direct survival of objects but also a continuing tradition of craftsmanship, usually centred on Constantinople but sometimes with strong streams flowing independently in the Roman or Arab worlds. There have also, again as in the case of sculpture and painting, been not infrequent revivals, when ancient models have been rediscovered, bringing ancient standards back into fashion.

HELLENISM

Hellenism has two senses. In the broader sense it characterises our whole civilisation as being descended from the Hellenic world. In this sense we are all Greeks, as Shelley said, and a visitor from another world who wanted to understand how Europe differed from, say, China, would eventually be driven to a study of ancient Greece; for that is where our art, science, and philosophy originated as well as much of our political and social morality.

The other, and more usual, sense of Hellenism is a partial one – the conscious love of ancient Greece and the desire to resurrect some or other aspect of it. In this sense of the word Hellenism has known many different manifestations, some contradictory. For instance, to the classicising critics of the early eighteenth century it meant obedience to the disciplines and refinements of Greek art; but in the Greek Revival a hundred years later it meant almost the opposite, and Byron could write of Don Juan and Haidée:

> . . . *they form a group that's quite antique,*
> *Half-naked, loving, natural, and Greek.*

The Platonism and Aristotelianism of the Middle Ages, though mutually opposed to each other, were both revivals of Greek thought. So was the Neoplatonism of the Renaissance. But Erasmus and his circle, though contemporary with the height of Neoplatonism, were Hellenists for a different reason. Their aim was not to revive a particular philosophy but a general style of simplicity, clarity, and truth. During the Reformation Greek was used as a lever against the Roman church. After that enthusiasm for it ebbed, only to flood to a new height in the Greek Revival at the end of the eighteenth century. A major, and rather surprising, consequence of this was the re-importation of ancient Greek into schools as a major subject of the curriculum, a rôle it maintained to within living memory. In England the authors taken most seriously were Plato and Thucydides, and a good case has been made for saying that these two ancient authors played a significant part in the administration of the British Empire when this was at its height. Two lesser but curious results of Hellenism have been the invention of opera (in intended revival of Greek tragedy) in Florence around the year 1600, and of rowing as a sport (in imitation of Athenian naval training) in English schools and universities in the early nineteenth century.

Hellenism in its first aspect as the distinguishing character of our civilisation is inescapable and as permanent as we are. In its revivalist sense, however, it is now at a low ebb. The proportion of educated people who can read ancient Greek is smaller than it was 100 years ago. On the other hand the archaeology of ancient Greece thrives as never before, there are probably as many professional Greek scholars as ever, and the knowledge at their disposal is more extensive, more accurate, and better organised than it has ever been. In short we know more about ancient Greece, and though the language may be less widely taught, there have never been so many readers of ancient Greek literature in translation or so many visitors to ancient Greek sites. This enthusiasm has not so far led to any coherent artistic, political, or educational movement. But the soil of Hellenism has proved fruitful beyond expectation on many occasions in the past, and it would be rash to predict that there are no more crops to come from it.

Sources

MODERN BOOKS

Chapter 1 The most useful and most recent English reference book to ancient civilisation in general is the Oxford Classical Dictionary (2nd ed, 1970). Fuller dictionaries exist for the specialist. The best bibliography of current classical studies is *L'Année philologique*, published annually in Paris, exhaustive but admirably easy to consult.

Chapter 2 **Early times:** D. R. Theocharis, *Neolithic Greece* (Athens, 1973); Colin Renfrew, *The emergence of civilisation: the Cyclades and the Aegean in the third millennium BC* (London, 1972). **Minoans:** Sinclair Hood, *The Minoans* (London, 1971); Reynold Higgins, *Minoan and Mycenaean art* (London, 1967). **Mycenaeans:** Lord William Taylour, *The Mycenaeans* (London, 1964); John Chadwick, *The decipherment of Linear B*, 2nd ed (Cambridge, 1967). **Dark Age:** A. M. Snodgrass, *The dark age of Greece: an archaeological survey of the eleventh to the eighth centuries BC* (Edinburgh, 1971); V. R. d'A. Desborough, *The Greek dark ages* (London, 1972). **Early colonisation:** John Boardman, *The Greeks overseas* (Harmondsworth, 1964); A. J. Graham, *Colony and mother-city in ancient Greece* (Manchester, 1964). **Greek world:** R. D. Milns, *Alexander the Great* (London, 1968); W. W. Tarn, *The Greeks in Bactria and India*, 2nd ed (Cambridge, 1951); A. K. Narain, *The Indo-Greeks* (Oxford, 1957); K. A. Nilakantra Sastri, *A history of South India*, 3rd ed (Oxford, 1966 – Ch 7, the Tamil poets); George Woodcock, *The Greeks in India* (London, 1966).

Chapter 3 **Language:** P. Chantraine, *Études sur le vocabulaire* *grec* (Paris, 1956); C. D. Buck, *The Greek dialects* (Chicago, 1955); L. Baumbach, *Studies in Mycenaean inscriptions and dialect: a bibliography* (Rome, 1968). **Religion:** H. J. Rose, *Ancient Greek religion* (London, 1946); E. R. Dodds, *The Greeks and the irrational* (Berkeley, 1951); F. C. Grant, *Hellenistic religions* (New York, 1953); G. E. Mylonas, *Eleusis and the Eleusinian mysteries* (Princeton, 1961); G. T. W. Hooker (ed), *Parthenos and Parthenon* (Oxford, 1963). **Legend and myth:** G. S. Kirk, *Myth: its meaning and functions in ancient and other cultures* (Cambridge, Berkeley, 1970). **Festivals:** H. A. Harris, *Greek athletes and athletics* (London, 1964). **Literacy and law:** L. H. Jeffery, *The local scripts of archaic Greece* (Oxford, 1963); E. G. Turner, *Athenian books in the 5th and 4th centuries BC* (London, 1952). **Olive and vine:** Peter Warren, *Myrtos: an early bronze age settlement in Crete* (London, 1972); L. G. Allbaugh, *Crete: a study of an underdeveloped area* (Princeton, 1953); Jane Renfrew, *Palaeoethnobotany: the prehistoric food plants of the near east and Europe* (London, 1973).

Chapter 4 **Historical perspectives:** R. Meiggs, *The Athenian Empire* (Oxford, 1972); G. E. M. de Ste Croix, *The origins of the Peloponnesian War* (Oxford, 1972); J. A. O. Larsen, *Greek federal states: their institutions and their history* (Oxford, 1968). **Democracy:** C. A. Hignett, *A history of the Athenian constitution to the end of the fifth century BC* (Oxford, 1952); W. G. G. Forrest, *The emergence of Greek democracy* (London, 1966); P. J. Rhodes, *The Athenian Boule* (Oxford, 1972); S. Dow, 'Aristotle, the Kleroteria, and the Courts' (*Harvard Stud in Class Phil*, 50 (1939), 1–34); F. G. Kenyon, *Aristotle on the constitution of Athens* (London, 1891). **Sparta and Crete:** W. G. G. Forrest, *A history of Sparta* (London, 1968); R. F. Willets, *Aristocratic society in ancient Crete* (London, 1955).

Chapter 5 **The working farmer:** W. E. Heitland, *Agricola* (Cambridge, 1921). **The landless man:** A. Burford, *Craftsmen in Greek and Roman society* (London, 1972). **The rich:** J. K. Davies, *Athenian propertied families 600–300 BC* (Oxford, 1971). **Women:** C. Seltman, *Women in antiquity* (London, 1956). **Slavery:** M. I. Finley (ed), *Slavery in classical antiquity: views* *and controversies* (Cambridge, 1960); A. W. Gomme, *The population of Athens in the 5th and 4th centuries BC* (Oxford, 1933); A. H. M. Jones, *Athenian democracy* (Oxford, 1957, pp 76–9 on population = *Econ Hist Rev*, 8, 1955, 142 ff); W. K. Pritchett (in *Hesperia*, 25, 1956, pp 276–81 on slave-prices). *Chapter 6* **Family life:** A. R. W. Harrison, *The law of Athens: the family and property* (Oxford, 1968); W. K. Lacey, *The family in classical Greece*; Anita Klein, *Child life in Greek art* (New York, 1932). **The house:** D. M. Robinson and J. W. Graham, *Excavations at Olynthus: part viii, The Hellenic House* (Baltimore, London, 1938); J. H. Young (in *Hesperia*, 25, 1956, 122 ff, farms); G. M. A. Richter, *The furniture of the Greeks, Etruscans, and Romans* (London, 1966); D. and P. Brothwell, *Food in antiquity: a survey of the diet of early peoples* (London, 1969). **Out of doors:** J. Delorme, *Gymnasion: étude sur les monuments consacrés à l'education en Grèce* (Paris, 1960).

Chapter 7 **Transport:** Alison Burford, *The Greek temple-builders at Epidaurus* (Liverpool, 1969); L. Casson, *Ships and seamanship in the ancient world* (Princeton, 1971); J. S. Morrison and R. T. Williams, *Greek oared ships: 900–322 BC* (Cambridge, 1968).

Chapter 8 **Archaic and classical education:** H. I. Marrou, *A history of education in antiquity*, tr G. Lamb (London, 1956); F. A. G. Beck, *Greek education 450–350 BC* (London, 1962).

Chapter 9 **Improvement:** M. I. Finley, 'Technical innovation and economic progress in the ancient world' (*Econ Hist Rev*, 1965, 29–45); A. Kleingünther, *Protos euretes* (Leipzig, 1933); Bacon, *Novum Organon*, I, 71, 85. **Primary production:** L. A. Moritz, *Grain-mills and flour in classical antiquity* (Oxford, 1958); R. J. Forbes, *Studies in ancient technology*, vol 2 (Leiden, 1955). **Arms and armour:** A. M. Snodgrass, *Arms and armour of the Greeks* (London, 1967); E. W. Marsden, *Greek and Roman artillery* (Oxford, 1969). **Buildings:** W. B. Dinsmoor, *The architecture of ancient Greece* (London, 1950). **Fine arts:** G. M. A. Richter, *Handbook of Greek art* (London, 1959); John Boardman, *Greek art* (London, 1964). **Mathematics and science:** T. L. Heath, *Greek mathematics* (Oxford, 1921); B.

Farrington, *Greek science* (Harmondsworth, 1953); M. Clagett, *Greek science in antiquity* (London, 1957); L. W. Daly, *Contributions to a history of alphabetisation* (Brussels, 1967); Gilbert Ryle, *Plato's Progress* (Cambridge, 1966, Ch 2 on festivals and books). *Chapter 10* **Language:** R. Browning, *Medieval and modern Greek* (London, 1969); W. W. Skeat, *Etymological Dictionary of the English Language* (1910). **Literature:** Albin Lesky, *A history of Greek literature*, Eng tr (London, 1966); H. C. Baldry, *Greek literature for the modern reader* (Cambridge, 1951). **Art:** See Ch 9. Also R. Lullies and Max Hirmer, *Greek Sculpture* (London, 1960); R. M. Cook, *Greek painted pottery* (London, 1960). **Hellenism:** G. Highet, *The classical tradition* (Oxford, 1949); R. M. Ogilvie, *Latin and Greek* (London, 1964).

REFERENCES TO ANCIENT AUTHORS

Homer, *Odyssey*, vi, 4–12; Strabo, II, 118; Hesiod, *Works and Days*, 648–59; Plato, *Ion*, 530 a–b, 535 c–e; Lysias, 33, 1–2; *Olympia: Ergebnisse*, V, 293 (Gorgias inscription); Euripides, *Supplices*, 433–4; Homer, *Iliad*, I, 157; Sophocles, *Antigone*, 332ff; Pliny, *Nat. Hist.*, 14, 150; Strabo, VIII, 8, 1 (comic poet on Megalopolis); Aristotle, *Politics*, IV, xi, 14 (1296a); VI, ii, 5–9 (1317b); Aristotle, *Politics*, VI, iv, 18 (1319b); Euripides, *Supplices*, 399–455; Lysias, 34, 5; Aristotle, *Politics*, IV, xi, 14 (1296a); [Xenophon], *Athenian Republic*, 5; Athenaeus, XV, 696 (song of Hybrias); Aristotle, *Politics*, II, i–vi (1261a–1266b); Aristophanes, *Plutus*, 903; Euripides, *Orestes*, 920; Homer, *Iliad*, XVIII, 550–60; Aristotle, *Politics*, IV, iv, 21 (1291b); Menander, *fr*, 62, Koerte; Homer, *Iliad*, XII, 310–28; [Demosthenes], 42, 22 (sanctimonious taxpayer); 50, 26 (the rat); [Demosthenes] 59, 22; Xenophon, *Memorabilia*, II, d 7 and [Demosthenes], 57, 47 (women earning); Demosthenes, 36, 14; 38, 6; 41, 17; 46, 57 (women financially *au fait*); Demosthenes, 39, 23 (family reconciliations); Herodotus, VI, 137 (slavery recent); Demosthenes, 33, 17–18; 34, 5–6 (slaves in positions of trust); [Demosthenes], 45 (Phormio's career); Xenophon, *Vectigalia*, iv, 4; Euripides, *fr*, 317; Aristotle,

Politics, VII, xvi (1334b); Aristotle, *Politics*, II, ix (1270a);
Panyassis, *fr*, 13 (libations); Theophrastus, *Characters*, 22, 10;
Hesiod, *Theogony*, 553; IG, I², 304A, 7; IG, II², 1635, 35–6;
Lysias, 1, 20; Menander, *Dyskolos*, 262; Theophrastus, *Charac-
ters*, 6 (loquacity), 13 (fussiness), 11 (coarseness), 9 (shameless-
ness), 5 (desire to please); Libanius, 61, 8–10; Xenophon,
Symposium, ad fin; Lysias, 24, 5; Machon, 389; Demosthenes,
21, 133 & 158; 42, 24; Homer, *Odyssey*, iii, 477–97; Herodotus,
ii, 17; vii, 176; Thucydides, ii, 100 (Macedonian roads);
Thucydides, iii, 68; Plato, *Laws*, xi, 918b; Theophrastus,
Characters, 6, 5; *Acts*, 27, 37; Josephus, *vita c Apionem*, 15;
Sallust, *Hist fr*, 8; Teles, *epit*, v; Aristotle, *Politics*, VIII, iii
(1337b); Xenophanes, *fr*, 2; Euripides, *fr*, 282; Plato, *Laws*,
ii, 654 a–b; Herodotus, vi, 27 (school at Chios); Pausanias, VI,
ix, 6 (school at Astypalaia); Theognis, 27ff; Teos inscriptions
in Michel, *Recueil*, 913 and Dittenberger, Sylloge, 578; Miletus
inscription in Dittenberger, *Sylloge*, 577; Homer, *Iliad*, IX,
440–4; Galen Protreptic, 3–5; Aeschylus, *Palamedes fr*, 303–4,
Mette; *PV*, 450; Euripides, *Supplices*, 201; Homeric Hymn, 20;
Gorgics, *fr*, 11a (30); Vitruvius, X, v, 2; *Anth Pal*, ix, 418;
Strabo, XII, 556; Aristotle, *Politics*, IV, xiii, 10 (1297b);
Xenophon, *Anabasis*, 6; Athenaeus, II, c 74 (Plato's clock);
Diogenes Laertius, V, 16 (Aristotle's alarm clock), Vitruvius,
IX, 9 (Ctesibius); Pliny, *Nat Hist*, 7, 60 (clock in Rome);
Anth Pal, vii, 641 (Athenaeus's clock); Petronius, *Sat*, 26, 9
(Trimalchio's clock); Lucian, *Hippias*, 8 (clock in the Baths);
Mon Germ Hist Auct Ant, XII, 39, 27 (Gundibald's clock);
Pliny, *Nat Hist*, 35, v 10 (story about Zeuxis).

The author and publishers are grateful to the following institutions and
individuals for supplying photographs and giving permission to reproduce
them: Ashmolean Museum, Oxford (Plates 1A, 2E, 4B, 6A, 8A–H);
Mr John Boardman (1B); the Trustees of the British Museum (4A, 6B);
Fitzwilliam Museum, Cambridge (4C); Girton College, Cambridge, (6D);
Hirmer Fotoarchiv, Munich (1C); Professor Morricone (2A–C); Staat-
liche Museen, Berlin (5A and B); Taranto Museum (6C).

Index

Aegina, 9
agriculture, 15, 71–2, 129, 131; *see also* food
Alexander the Great, 14, 29, 47, 134
Alexandria, 14, 29, 126, 153
Al Mina, 23
alphabet, 40–1, 122; *see also* writing
alphabetic order, 142
anchors, 111, 137
Antioch, 14, 29
Antiphilus of Byzantium, 138
Aphrodite, 97, 114
Apollo, 33, 35
arch, 136
Argonauts, 36, 77
Aristarchus of Samos, 141
Aristophanes, 151; cited, 71
Aristotle, 78, 152; his school at the Lykeion, 78, 99, 126–7; on systems of government, 52–3, 64, 65, 69, 132; influence of his political views, 65, 69; on Sparta, 63, 91; on slavery, 79; on marriage, 89, 91; on education, 117–18; on Homer's *Odyssey*, 149
Artemis, 43
artillery, 133–5
Assembly, in Athens, 52, 54, 55, 56, 66
astronomy, 140–1
Athena, 10, 33, 35
Athens, 12; size, 46, 82; empire, 47; navy, 112–13; the Athenian democracy, 53–70; manners and society, 98, 100–2; as educational centre, 126; pottery, 21, 155–6, *51*; coinage, 9, *104*; plan of centre, 57
athletics, 98, 100, 118–19, 124–5, *68*; *see also* Games
Attic, *see* Athens

Bacon, Francis, 128
Bactria, 10, 14, 29
banking, 80–1

books, 121–3, 143, 147, 152–3
bottomry loans, *see* shipping
boulē, see Council
Bronze Age Greece, 13–19, 21–2, 33 44–5
building materials, 92–3
Byron, 154, 158
Byzantium, Byzantine, 12, 13–14, 28, 136, 157

Cargoes, *see* shipping
Carthaginians, 25, 133, 136
Catane, 12, 27
cavalry at Athens, 55, 75, 107
children, *see* family life, schools
Choerilus of Samos, 150
Christian literature, 153
citizens and citizenship, 48, 54, 71–9, 82, 112, 128–9
city-state, 46–8, 51
Cleisthenes, 53
clocks, 137–9; in law-courts, 59, 61
colonisation, 23–30
comedy, 89, 93, 100, 151–2
Constantinople, *see* Byzantium
Corcyra, 12, 27
Corinth, 12, 27, 109, 133, *67*
Council, in Athens, 54–7, 65
crafts and craftsmen, prehistoric, 15, 16, 19–20; classical, 72–3, 78–9, 127; Greek crafts in India, 30; relationship with religion, 35, 129; survival, 154–5, 157
Crete, 12; in the Bronze Age, 15–18, 21, 44–5; in historic times, 23, 44–5, 62–4, 97
Ctesibius, 138
Cycladic culture, 16
Cynics, 88, 117
Cyprus, 20, 21
Cyrene, 24, 28, 53
Cyzicus, 9, 12